ASSEMBLY LANGUAGE BASICS
An Annotated Program Book

Hayden Computer Programming Series

James N. Haag, Consulting Editor
Professor of Computer Science and Physics
University of San Francisco

COMPREHENSIVE STANDARD FORTRAN PROGRAMMING
James N. Haag

COMPREHENSIVE FORTRAN PROGRAMMING
James N. Haag

BASICS OF DIGITAL COMPUTER PROGRAMMING (Rev. 2nd Ed.)
John S. Murphy

BASIC BASIC: An Introduction to Computer Programming in BASIC Language
James S. Coan

DISCOVERING BASIC: A Problem Solving Approach
Robert E. Smith

BEGINNING FORTRAN: Simplified, 12-Statement Programming
John Maniotes, Harry B. Higley, and James N. Haag

ASSEMBLY LANGUAGE BASICS: An Annotated Program Book
Irving A. Dodes

PROGRAMMING PROVERBS
Henry F. Ledgard

PROGRAMMING PROVERBS FOR FORTRAN PROGRAMMERS
Henry F. Ledgard

ASSEMBLY LANGUAGE BASICS
An Annotated Program Book

Irving Allen Dodes, Ph.D.
Professor of Mathematics
Kingsborough College
The City University of New York

HAYDEN BOOK COMPANY, INC.
Rochelle Park, New Jersey

Library of Congress Cataloging in Publication Data

Dodes, Irving Allen.
   Assembly language basics.

  (Hayden computer programming series)
   1. Assembler language (Computer program language)
2. Computer programs. I. Title.
QA76.73.A8D62   001.6'425   74-22039
ISBN 0-8104-5989-2

Copyright © 1975 by HAYDEN BOOK COMPANY, INC. All rights reserved. No part of this book may be reprinted, or reproduced, or utilized in any form or by any electronic, mechanical, or other means, now known or hereafter invented, including photocopying and recording, or in any information storage and retrieval system, without permission in writing from the Publisher.

Printed in the United States of America

    1 2 3 4 5 6 7 8 9   PRINTING

75 76 77 78 79 80 81 82   YEAR

Preface

This book has a very modest, limited purpose: to display samples of simple programs in the basic Assembly language (BAL) of the IBM 360/370 system. The fourteen sample programs have been chosen to illustrate input-output (I/O), IBM error messages, binary addition (unedited), the partial dump ("snapshot" or "bus-stop") method for debugging, minor editing, editing using EDMK, binary multiplication, binary division, decimal arithmetic operations, the solution of a simple formula requiring several skills, the use of tape and disk for "scratch," address modification, and one method of sorting within core.

In the very first program, all the output sheets are shown with an explanation of the symbols on them. In the second program, the PRINT NOGEN instruction is omitted in order to show exactly what the computer is doing; at the same time, some common error messages are shown. After that, the computer output display is limited to the most useful parts.

It should be noted that *job control* and *file definition* cards differ somewhat from installation to installation. This should occasion no great difficulty; ordinarily, each Computer Center publishes a statement explaining the form of job control and file definition cards required by the specific model and determined by options at SYSGEN time.

The introductory remarks for each program tell the purpose of the program and the new concept to be illustrated. In a few cases, a *flowchart* (block diagram) has been drawn to illuminate the logic.

Each instruction is explained in the Appendix, and at least one illustration is given of the application of the instruction. The Appendix is in lieu of an index.

The author has taught programming, including machine language, assembly languages, and various compiler languages, since 1950. In each case, the most effective teaching device proved to be demonstration programs.

This set of sample programs does *not* replace a regular textbook, a reference manual, or the teacher's notes. It is, and is intended to be, a way to get the student started on something which is really quite difficult at the beginning. It is hoped that this aim will be satisfied.

Irving Allen Dodes

New York

Contents

Program One
A Simple Input-Output Program 1

Program Two
Program to Illustrate Some Error Messages 9

Program Three
Adding Three Numbers (Binary) 19

Program Four
Snapshot Method (Partial Dumps) 23

Program Five
Addition in Binary with Minor Editing 29

Program Six
Binary Addition with EDMK 33

Program Seven
Binary Multiplication 41

Program Eight
Binary Division with EDMK and Half-Adjustment 45

Program Nine
Simple Formula 49

Program Ten
Use of Tape for Scratch 54

Program Eleven
Use of Scratch Disk (WORKA Method) 62

Program Twelve
Use of Scratch Disk (IOREG Method) 69

Program Thirteen
Address Modification 73

Program Fourteen
Program to Demonstrate Internal Sorting and Address Modification 78

Appendix for Instructions 82
    Classes of Instructions 82
    Macro-Instructions 82
    Categories of Simple Instructions 83
    Abbreviations 83
    Table for 99 Selected Fixed-Point Instructions 84
    Group I. Loading Binary Numbers 84
    Group II. Storing Binary Numbers 85
    Group III. Binary Arithmetic Instructions 86
    Group IV. Arithmetic Shifts 88
    Group V. "Move" Instructions 88
    Group VI. Changing the Form of a Number 89
    Group VII. Decimal Arithmetic Instructions 90
    Group VIII. "Compare" Instructions 91
    Group IX. "Branch" Instructions 92
    Group X. Special "Branch" Instructions 95
    Group XI. Logical Arithmetic 96
    Group XII. Logical Shift Instructions 97
    Group XIII. Other Logical Instructions 98
    Group XIV. Editing Instructions 101

ASSEMBLY LANGUAGE BASICS
An Annotated Program Book

Program One

A Simple Input-Output Program

In all the printouts, some of the lines of print begin with an asterisk in card column (cc) 1. This can be seen throughout the programs in this book. These cards, identified by an * and a blank in the first two columns, are called *comment cards*. They are inserted as aids to the programmer:

    to make explanations
    to separate portions of the program
    to use as headings for parts of the program.

In any case, the computer pays no attention to them, so to speak. It merely prints them.

It is very important to have a program clear to the reader, not only at the time it is written, but (more importantly) some time later when the programmer has possibly forgotten why certain things were done. There is a way of making comments for individual instructions, as well. This will be demonstrated in all the later programs in the book.

The first cards are *job control cards* which tell the computer

    the name of the program
    which "options" are desired
    which language will be used.

The main purpose of the first job control card is to notify the computer that a new job is on its way. Unfortunately, the JCL (job control language) of job control cards is not uniform.

In this installation (where the programs were run), a job control card is identified by a double slash, //, in cc 1 and 2 and a blank in column 3. The first job control card is, then,

// JOB ONE

The *options* also vary from one place to another. At SYSGEN ("system generation") time, the computer center selects certain options as standard, i.e., unless the programmer says he doesn't want them, they are assumed to be wanted. Among these are options like LOG (list the program on the console typewriter) and LIST (list the programs and all the steps on the output device). If the computer center had *not* made these standard, the second job card in Program ONE would have been

// OPTION LINK,LOG,LIST

At this installation, a listing could have been prevented by specifying

// OPTION LINK,NOLIST

The IBM manual specific to your installation has a directory of options.

The third job control card in Program ONE specifies the language which the programmer is using. If the language had been FORTRAN, this card would have been

// EXEC FORTRAN

Here again, there is not necessarily uniformity from one installation to the next. For example, the computer center may specify a different spelling, e.g., ASSEMBLF for "full assembler" or FOR for FORTRAN.

There are many other job control cards, and some of them will be explained in the fourteen programs within this book. For a full set specific to your installation, a reference manual is essential.

On page 5 are shown the first two pages of an IBM printout for the first program. The first page had only four lines, consisting of three job control cards and a comment card. The second page of the printout had the External Symbol Dictionary (ESD). Under ID it can be seen that there were three *control sections*, numbered 01, 02, and 03. This page is of little or no importance to the beginning programmer and will not be shown in the rest of the book. It is interesting, however, that the computer keeps its own "dictionary" to keep track of the parts of the job. Advanced programmers find the ESD useful in finding certain errors.

Page 6 is the actual program listing. The right side of the listing (beginning at the double line) is an exact copy of the input cards. Each line with a card number at the right is a *card image*, except for statements 99-102, which are inserted by the Assembler. Starting at the double line, the IBM heading is SOURCE STATEMENT. The symbol at the right tells the *level* of Assembler used, in this case the "F" level for a *disk-operated system* (DOS). Right of that is the date on which the program was run.

Remember that the first few cards were job control cards and a comment card. After these cards, the next two cards were comment cards, inserted to explain what the program was about. The purpose of this program couldn't be simpler: merely to read a card and print its contents (making this the most expensive typewriter in the world). The process is called *input-output*, usually referred to as I/O.

The next card was

PRINT NOGEN

which is almost always found in an Assembler program. To explain this, look at the heading STMT (*statement*) just to the left of the double line. In general, the computer numbers the statements, starting at 1 and going up to 65,535. Looking down the STMT column, note that the numbers increase by 1 until statement 6, when there is a sudden jump to 27. This is not a mistake. What this means is that our instruction DTFCD ("Define the file as a cardfile") required the Assembler to translate one line into 21 different instructions. Because the computer never makes a mistake, the programmer ordinarily has no interest in these *generated instructions*. The instruction

PRINT NOGEN

means, "Do not print the generated instructions." In Program TWO, this command will be omitted to show the instructions generated by the computer.

The START card sets the location counter to the (hex) value shown in the operand (which is in decimal). In this case, there was no operand and the computer assumed zero (0). At the left, note 000000 under LOC. If this card had had the operand 256 (which is decimal), the location counter would have been set to 100, which is the hex equivalent. In general, there is no point in specifying a starting point.

The next card is a comment card which tells that the two cards which follow are there to define files. In this case, the cardfile (CARDF) is defined by a DTFCD. There are only three operands in this case, to answer the questions:

what device is the information coming from?
where shall it be put?
what shall be done when there are no more data?

for which the answers are: the card reader (SYSRDR), the area which the programmer has set aside as CARD (see statement 86), and "perform the instruction which the programmer has decided to call INEND" (see statement 73).

The other file definition is the DTFPR for the *printer* (SYSLST). In this text, there will be other DTF's (for magnetic tape, and for disk). Each has its own requirements. The DTFPR asks:

on what device shall the information be printed?
how long is a print line?
where is the information coming from?

for which the answers are: on the printer; 132 bytes; "get it from the area designated by the programmer as PRTOUT" (see statement 90). At this point, the programmer might be puzzled by the first question. Isn't it obvious that the output device is a printer? There are several reasons for the question and answer, one of which is that there may be several printers and the device used may be identified by some other name.

File definitions may differ from one installation to another depending upon the "standard" adopted at SYSGEN time and upon the kind of operating system in the installation, i.e., DOS, TOS, OS, or VS. Also, there are many other I/O options available, some of which will be shown in later programs.

The next section of the program is the *Housekeeping Section*. At the moment, in this simple program, the only things that are done are to designate a *base register* (by statements 49 and 50) and to instruct the computer to open the channels to the two files described in CARDF and PRINTF, namely the card reader and the printer. In later programs, other "housekeeping" (having to do with neatness of output) will be shown.

The actual program procedure really consists of a GET, two MVCs and a PUT. It is important to know that

GET CARDF

reads exactly *one* card, and

PUT PRINTF

prints precisely *one* line. The MVC is explained in the Appendix, where all the simple instructions are explained and illustrated with actual examples.

Note that the *Procedure Section* ends with an instruction to close the channels and with

EOJ

which informs the computer that the procedural parts of the program are finished.

The programmer should write the program and the associated data areas at the same time, but it is convenient to put all the designated data areas together at the end, after the EOJ. Note that the program as a whole must end with an END card, and the operand of the END card must be the label of the BALR instruction.

At some point, a programmer must learn to read the machine translation of his assembly instructions. Look at statement 67. Using the green card (IBM Reference Data form GX20-1703), note that MVC is an SS instruction translated as D2. From the Appendix of this book, it will be seen that MVC is an SS1, meaning that the lengths of both operands are given by the length specified in the first operand. The first operand is ADDOUT which (according to statement 94) has a (decimal) length of 35. The way the machine was built, this length is *reduced by one* and the result is converted to hex. But 34_{10} = 22_x. So far, this explains D222. The B0D5 should be the base-displacement address of ADDOUT. The *B* is simply hex for (decimal) 11, which was designated as the base register in statements 49 and 50. The 0D5 is the displacement found in this case, by subtracting the location of the USING (00006A) from the location of ADDOUT (00013F). If the USING had been written as

USING NEXT,11

then the location of NEXT (whatever that turned out to be) would have been used to subtract. An example of this is in Program THIRTEEN.

The reader should now verify B067 as the base-displacement address of ADDRESS.

Following the Program ONE listing, there are *seven* pages, some having only a single line of print. Of course, in a complicated program, the pages might all be filled with material of greater or lesser value to the programmer, particularly if there is an error in the program. (There is almost always an error in the program the first few times, even for a very experienced programmer.)

The RELOCATION DICTIONARY is of little or no value to the beginning programmer. It contains information needed by the computer to "find" control sections, address constants, etc.

The CROSS-REFERENCE section is of great importance in checking a program, as will be seen in Program TWO. The machine keeps an excellent record of where every symbol was defined and all the places it was used (referenced). The symbols preceded by IJ are IBM-supplied programs which are automatically included with the programmer's program. Ordinarily they are of no interest to the programmer. They become of interest if the program was "called" and, for some reason, does not exist on the machine. Then the computer director should be notified so that he can insert the program which, in turn, will be linked to the user's program.

The next page has only one entry:

// EXEC LNKEDT

This is a JCL card image (the 29th card) which calls in the link-editing program which puts all the pieces together.

The *map* on the next page of the printout is of little or no use for elementary programs, but the page following that one is useful in *debugging* (correcting) a program. The use will be shown in Program TWO. The next page of the printout has the JCL command

// EXEC

which was the card following card 290. This means "go ahead and execute the program."

There was one data card, with its format described in the comment at the beginning of the program listing (statements 1 and 2). Following the one data card was a card with /* in cc 1 and 2. This told the computer that the previous card was the *end of data*. The last card of the program was / & which told the computer that this was the *end of the job*.

Notice that the result of the program was to print a name and address immediately after the / / EXEC. This is definitely unsatisfactory and will be handled more usefully in later programs by *control instructions*.

```
// JOB ONE          ← The name of the job.
* A SIMPLE INPUT-OUTPUT (I/O) PROGRAM    The * in card column 1      11.58.48  ← The job was run at almost 11:59 A.M.
// OPTION LINK                           makes this a "comment card."
// EXEC ASSEMBLY                                                      020
                                                                      030
```

// OPTION LINK — This program was to be link-edited for temporary use. A program kept in the computer for frequent use would have CATAL (for "catalog") instead of LINK.

EXEC ASSEMBLY — This names the language being used.

Symbols that appear in the name field of a START or a CSECT ("control section"). In this case, ONE is the name in front of START (statement 4, next page). The other two are IBM-supplied control sections used for file definition. This program has three sections to be linked.

EXTERNAL SYMBOL DICTIONARY   PAGE   1

```
SYMBOL    TYPE ID  ADDR    LENGTH  LD ID
ONE       SD   01  000000  0001A8
IJCFZIZ0   ER   02
IJDFZZZZ   ER   03
```

Type: SD = section definition, ER = external reference. Other
"types" are: LD = entry
              PC = private code
              CM = Common control section
              WX = weak external reference

ID: identification number used by the machine

ADDR: the hex location of the control section.

LENGTH: The hex length of the control section. $1A8_x = 1 \times 16^2 + 10 \times 16^1 + 8 \times 16^0 = 256 + 160 + 8 = 424_{10}$ bytes.

LD ID: If there is an LD, its ID.

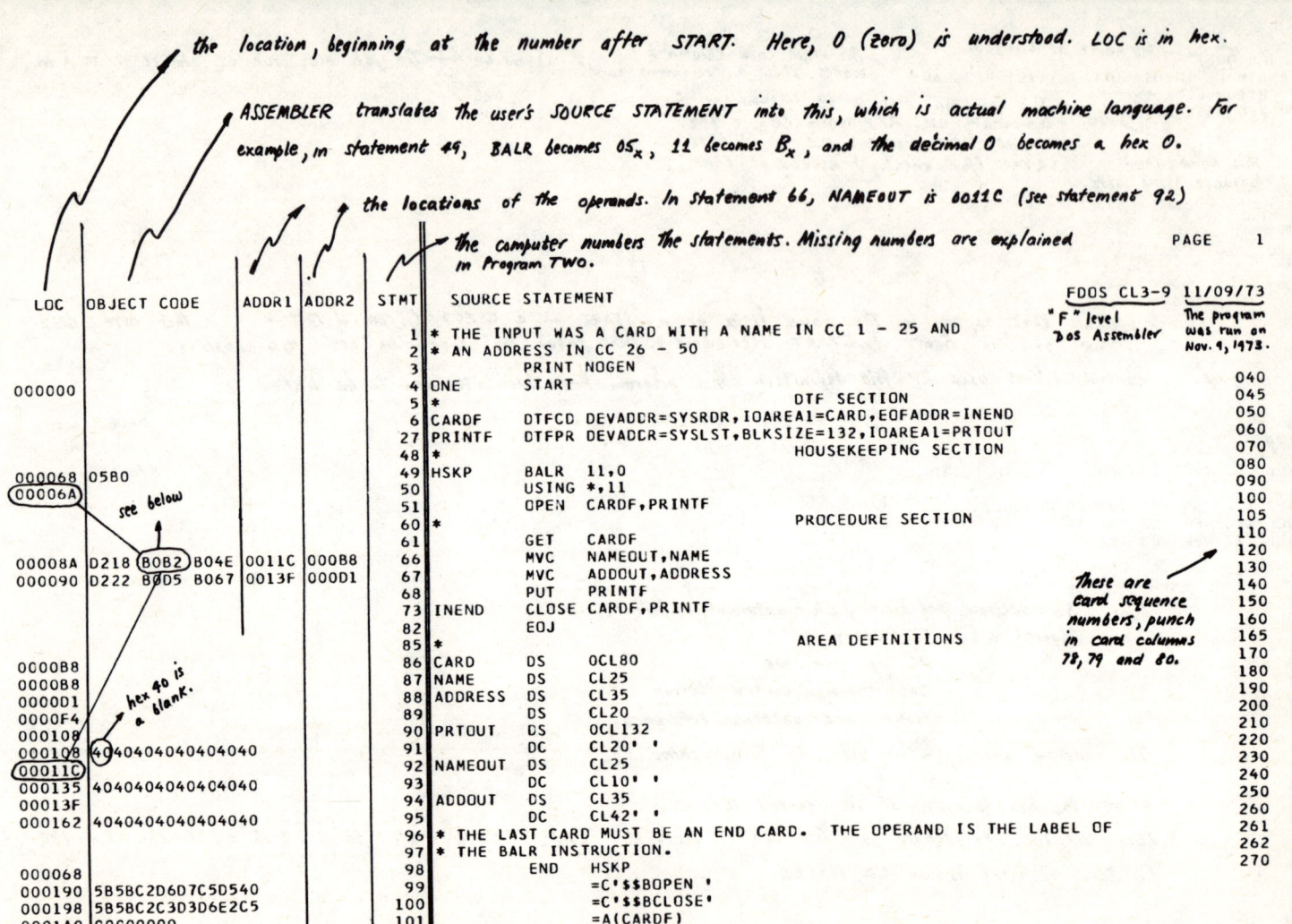

the location, beginning at the number after START. Here, 0 (zero) is understood. LOC is in hex.

ASSEMBLER translates the user's SOURCE STATEMENT into this, which is actual machine language. For example, in statement 49, BALR becomes 05_x, 11 becomes B_x, and the decimal 0 becomes a hex 0.

the locations of the operands. In statement 66, NAMEOUT is 0011C (see statement 92)

the computer numbers the statements. Missing numbers are explained in Program TWO.

PAGE 1

FDOS CL3-9 11/09/73
"F" level DOS Assembler
The program was run on Nov. 9, 1973.

```
LOC      OBJECT CODE      ADDR1  ADDR2   STMT   SOURCE STATEMENT
                                           1   * THE INPUT WAS A CARD WITH A NAME IN CC 1 - 25 AND        040
                                           2   * AN ADDRESS IN CC 26 - 50                                 045
                                           3           PRINT NOGEN                                        050
000000                                     4   ONE     START                                              060
                                           5   *                              DTF SECTION                 070
                                           6   CARDF   DTFCD DEVADDR=SYSRDR,IOAREA1=CARD,EOFADDR=INEND    080
                                          27   PRINTF  DTFPR DEVADDR=SYSLST,BLKSIZE=132,IOAREA1=PRTOUT    090
                                          48   *                              HOUSEKEEPING SECTION        100
000068   05B0                             49   HSKP    BALR  11,0                                         105
00006A                                    50           USING *,11                                         110
                                          51           OPEN  CARDF,PRINTF                                 120
                                          60   *                              PROCEDURE SECTION           130
                                          61           GET   CARDF                                        140
00008A   D218 B0B2 B04E  0011C  000B8     66           MVC   NAMEOUT,NAME                                 150
000090   D222 B0D5 B067  0013F  000D1     67           MVC   ADDOUT,ADDRESS                               160
                                          68           PUT   PRINTF                                       165
                                          73   INEND   CLOSE CARDF,PRINTF                                 170
                                          82           EOJ                                                180
                                          85   *                              AREA DEFINITIONS            190
0000B8                                    86   CARD    DS    0CL80                                        200
0000B8                                    87   NAME    DS    CL25                                         210
0000D1                                    88   ADDRESS DS    CL35                                         220
0000F4                                    89           DS    CL20                                         230
000108                                    90   PRTOUT  DS    0CL132                                       240
000108   4040404040404040                 91           DC    CL20' '                                      250
00011C                                    92   NAMEOUT DS    CL25                                         260
000135   4040404040404040                 93           DC    CL10' '                                      261
00013F                                    94   ADDOUT  DS    CL35                                         262
000162   4040404040404040                 95           DC    CL42' '                                      270
                                          96   * THE LAST CARD MUST BE AN END CARD.  THE OPERAND IS LABEL OF
                                          97   * THE BALR INSTRUCTION.
000068                                    98           END   HSKP
000190   5B5BC2D6D7C5D540                 99                 =C'$$BOPEN '
000198   5B5BC2C3D3D6E2C5                100                 =C'$$BCLOSE'
0001A0   00C00000                        101                 =A(CARDF)
0001A4   00C00038                        102                 =A(PRINTF)
```

see below

hex 40 is a blank.

These are card sequence numbers, punch in card columns 78, 79 and 80.

B0B2 in statement 66 is the base-displacement address of NAMEOUT. The first "B" is hex for (register 11) which was designated in statements 49 and 50. The displacement is $0B2_x$ found by subtracting: The location of NAMEOUT (= $11C_x$) minus the location of USING (= $06A_x$).

6

RELOCATION DICTIONARY   PAGE   1

```
POS.ID   REL.ID   FLAGS   ADDRESS
  01       01      0C     000008
  01       02      18     000011
  01       01      0C     000018
  01       01      0C     00001C
  01       01      08     000021
  01       01      0C     000040
  01       03      18     000049
  01       01      0C     000050
  01       01      08     000061
  01       01      0C     000074
  01       01      0C     000078
  01       01      0C     0000AC
  01       01      0C     0000B0
  01       01      0C     0001A0
  01       01      0C     0001A4
```

                                                                                               11/09/73

POS.ID : *Identification number (from the External Symbol Dictionary, ESD) for a control section (CS) in which an address constant is an operand.*

REL.ID : *ID from ESD for a CS in which the referenced symbol is defined.*

FLAGS : *Two hex digits. The first describes the type of address constant. The second contains its length and sign.*

ADDRESS : *The address where the address constant is stored. For example, see statement 102, at location 0001A4. The address of PRINTF is at that location.*

CROSS-REFERENCE   PAGE   1
                                                                                               11/09/73

```
SYMBOL     LEN    VALUE   DEFN    REFERENCES
ADDOUT    C0035  00013F  00094    0067
ADDRESS   C0035  00C0D1  C0088    0067
CARD      C0080  000088  C0086    0020  0022
CARDF     C0006  00C000  00009    0057  0063  0079  0101
HSKP      C0002  000068  00049    0098
IJCX0001  C0008  00C020  C0022    0012
IJJC0006  C0004  0000A8  C0078
IJJ00003  C0004  000070  C0056
IJJZ0001  C0001  000032  C0026
IJJZ0002  C0001  000068  C0047
INEND     C0004  0000A4  C0076    0021
NAME      C0025  000088  C0087    0066
NAMEOUT   C0025  00011C  C0092    0066
ONE       C0001  000000  C0004
PRINTF    C0006  00C038  C0030    0058  0070  0080  0102
PRTOUT    C0132  000108  C0090    0041  0046
```

SYMBOL: *The name assigned either by the user or by Assembler.*

LEN: *Length (in decimal). For example, see statement 94, where ADDOUT is defined with length = 35 bytes.*

VALUE: *Either the location or the actual value (in hex).*

DEFN: *Where it was first defined. CARD is defined in statement 86.*

REFERENCES: *Where else it is used. CARD is used in statements 20 and 22, not shown because of statement 3. Now, look at NAME.*

NO STATEMENTS FLAGGED IN THIS ASSEMBLY →

If there had been syntax errors, a section called "Diagnostics" would have been printed. Program TWO shows this.

`// EXEC LNKEDT` — *This calls in Link-Editor which hooks all the control sections together and gets the program ready for execution.*

```
JOB ONE      11/09/73    DISK LINKAGE EDITOR DIAGNOSTIC OF INPUT
ACTION TAKEN   MAP
LIST   AUTOLINK   IJCFZIZO
LIST   AUTOLINK   IJDFZZZZ
LIST   ENTRY
```

This is a record, in "map" form, of what Link-Editor did. The map becomes important in complicated programs using COMMON, PHASE, ROOT, INCLUDE.

beginning and end of core addresses — LOCORE, HICORE
where the control section actually began (in hex).
relocation factor. For the simple programs, the same as LOADED.

```
11/09/73  PHASE  XFR-AD  LOCORE  HICORE  DSK-AD    ESD TYPE  LABEL     LOADED  REL-FR
          PHASE*** 002868 002800  002A37  5C 02 1   CSECT     ONE       002800  002800
                                                    CSECT     IJCFZIZO  0029A8  0029A8
                                                    CSECT     IJDFZZZZ  002A10  002A10
```

Cylinder, head, record — disk address

`// EXEC` ← *instruction to run the program which was link-edited.*

```
         I.A.DUDES                      KINGSBOROUGH COLLEGE
```
← *OUTPUT OF PROGRAM*

"End of job"
`EOJ ONE`

when it ended   *It took 1 minute and 48 seconds.*
`12.00.36,DURATION 00.01.48`
hr. / min. / sec.

8

Program Two

Program to Illustrate Some Error Messages

This program is similar to Program ONE and has two purposes: (1) to demonstrate what the computer does when an error is detected, and (2) to demonstrate *computer-generated instructions* by omitting the PRINT NOGEN card.

In general, omission of the PRINT NOGEN card is not a good idea, mainly because it makes the program very hard to read. In the listing that follows, each user's instruction is shown by an arrow. All the others were written by the Assembler program. Note the + symbol following the statement numbers for computer-generated instructions.

When the computer finds an error, it prints

*** ERROR ***

after the instruction which contains the error. In some cases, the computer is able to recognize a typographical error and correct it with no fuss. This is called *correction by default* and usually results in a kind of memo called an MNOTE (see statement 68 under DIAGNOSTICS).

Not all errors are found by the machine. For example, look at statements 94 and 100. Statement 94 was impossible on the machine used because 60,000 bytes, plus the other bytes needed, would not fit. However, it is possible to compile a program on a small machine and run it on a larger one, so the computer did not "consider" this an error. If the program had had no other errors, the computer would have tried to run it. At that time, the error would have been identified and an error message printed. In statement 100, there was a logical error, i.e., the length was wrong. There was no way the computer could find a logical error. To summarize, the computer can find errors in spelling, in grammar, and in syntax, but not errors in logic.

Going to the beginning of the listing, note that DUMP has been included as an option. This means, "If an error occurs when the program is executed, print out the *complete* contents of core." This is a slow and wasteful process. A much better method is the *partial dump*, to be shown in Program FOUR. However, everyone ought to see it once. For this reason, pages 1 and 5 of the dump are reproduced for the reader. It is really hard to read, used by experts only *in emergency*. On page 17 note that the dump begins with a display of the contents of the 16 general-purpose registers, the 4 floating-point registers, and the address of the communication region. Register 11 has 2810_x in it. The first 2800_x bytes contain the supervisor and various saved items, like the date. The date, in zoned format, appears twice, once at 000288_x (with slashes) and again at $0002D7$ (without the slashes). Where a combination of symbols makes sense in the EBCDIC representation, it is translated at the right. Otherwise, dots appear.

The program, itself, begins after the supervisor. On page 18, the comment (beginning with the blank) is shown by brackets and, below, the BALR instruction of the user's program, translated as 05B0, is shown at 002868. This is the actual address of the instruction, found by adding the relocation factor (2800_x in this installation) to the location for statement 47, namely 000068, found under the column LOC on page 12.

Before turning to an explanation of how the IBM output can be used to debug a program, look at statement 1. This statement contains a comment written by the programmer:

(THIS IS THE LETTER. IT SHOULD BE 0.)

Two things should be noted: (1) Any instruction can have a comment. The comment is recognized by leaving one or more blanks after the instruction. (2) *Never* leave blanks in the operands. If you do, everything after the blank will be regarded as a comment. For example, the instruction

MVC NAME,NAMEOUT

will be translated correctly, but

MVC NAME, NAMEOUT

will be an error because Assembler will read the instruction as

MVC NAME,

and will consider NAMEOUT as a comment because of the space.

Returning to statement 1, suppose a hard look did not reveal that the letter, O, had been used in place of the number, 0. The computer claims that this is an error. Turn to the DIAGNOSTICS, page 16. Under statement 1, the computer tells that the near operand is wrong. This should be enough of a hint.

Look at statement 18+. If the PRINT NOGEN statement had been included, as it normally is, the *** ERROR *** would have appeared after statement 3 since the statements generated would not have been printed. In this case, it is clear that the trouble is with FINIS, for some reason. Looking at CROSS-REFERENCE on page 15, we see that FINIS was used in statement 18 but never defined. However, right under it, FINISH was defined but never used. In other words, statement 3 should have included

EOFADDR=FINISH

This is typical of debugging for this type of error. Use the statement number, then the DIAGNOSTICS and the CROSS-REFERENCE together.

There are error messages after user's statements 64 and 65. For statement 64, DIAGNOSTICS says that the operation code is undefined. Upon looking at it, the programmer should see that CONTROL should have been spelled CNTRL. In statement 65, the operation code is spelled correctly, but (as can be seen by looking under statement 68 in DIAGNOSTICS) SKIP should have been SK.

Statement 72 represents a typical error. The programmer types PIT for PUT and forgets to remove the incorrect card. DIAGNOSTICS locates the error.

Statement 73 is the kind of error that shows the computer is only a machine. According to DIAGNOSTICS, the address OUTPRT is unsatisfactory. When we look at the instruction, it seems to be perfectly all right. According to CROSS-REFERENCE, there doesn't seem to be any problem. Where is the trouble? The trouble is that the computer was unable to put together OUTPRT properly because there is an error elsewhere. Actually, there is nothing wrong with statement 73.

It is a good exercise to go through the listing to find the real and not-so-real errors. Remember that if something is defined incorrectly, or not defined at all, or misspelled, all the instructions which have this thing in it will be marked as errors, even if they are not. The other thing to remember is that when the PRINT NOGEN is in, as it should be (except maybe once), the statement number under DIAGNOSTICS and CROSS-REFERENCE may be confusing until you get used to it.

On page 16, the last page of the IBM printout is shown. There are two lines on it. The first line tells that Job TWO was canceled due to an invalid address (the first address it couldn't find, because of an error). The second line contains the *Program Status Word* (PSW). Refer to the green card for a complete explanation of this word. The ninth character, here a 1, tells why the program was interrupted, and the right end sometimes tells the instruction address where the interrupt occurred. This is occasionally useful when the interruption code is due to an overflow or underflow or loss of significance.

```
// JOB TWO                                                    12.00.43
* PROGRAM TO ILLUSTRATE SOME ERROR MESSAGES
// OPTION LINK,(DUMP)   → an option to              020
// EXEC ASSEMBLY          be avoided.               030
```

an option to be avoided.

PAGE   1

```
     LOC   OBJECT CODE     ADDR1 ADDR2   STMT    SOURCE STATEMENT                                      FDOS CL3-9 11/09/73

   000000                              → 1 TWO       START 0    (THIS IS THE LETTER. IT SHOULD BE 0.)         050
         *** ERROR ***
                                       → 2 *                                DTF SECTION                        060
                                       → 3 INCARDS   DTFCD DEVADDR=SYSRDR,IOAREA1=CARD,EOFADDR=FINIS          070
                                         4+* 360N-CL-453   DTFCD   CHANGE LEVEL 3-10                    3-10
   000000                                 5+              DC     0D'0'
   000000 00C080000000                    6+INCARDS       DC     X'000080000000' RES. COUNT,COM. BYTES,STATUS BTS
   000006 00                              7+              DC     AL1(0) LOGICAL UNIT CLASS.
   000007 00                              8+              DC     AL1(0) LOGICAL UNIT
   000008 00C00020                        9+              DC     A(IJCX0001) CCW ADDRESS
   00000C 00C00000                       10+              DC     4X'00' CCB-ST BYTE,CSW CCW ADDR.
   000010 00                             11+              DC     AL1(0) 3-3
   000011 00C000                         12+              DC     VL3(IJCFZIZO) ADDRESS OF LOGIC MODULE     3-3
   000014 02                             13+              DC     X'02' DTF TYPE (READER)
   000015 01                             14+              DC     AL1(1) SWITCHES
   000016 02                             15+              DC     AL1(2) NORMAL COMM.CODE
   000017 02                             16+              DC     AL1(2) CNTROL COMM.CODE
   000018 00C000B8                       17+              DC     A(CARD) ADDR. OF IOAREA1
   00001C 00C00000                       18+              DC     A(FINIS) EOF ADDRESS                    3-8
         *** ERROR ***
   000020 02C000B820000050               19+IJCX0001  CCW    2,CARD,X'20',80
   000028 47C0 0000              00000   20+           NOP    0 LOAD USER POINTER REG.
   00002C 47C0 0000              00000   21+           NOP    0 MOVE IOAREA TO WORKA
   000030 0000                           22+           DC     X'0000'
   000032                                23+IJJZ0001  EQU    *
                                       →24 OUTPRT     DTFPR BLKSIZE=232,DEVADDR=SYSLST,IOAREA1=PRTOUT         090
                                         25+* 360 N-CL-453   DTFPR   CHANGE LEVEL 3-9                    3-9
                                         26                   0,BLKSIZE GREATER THAN 132 132 ASSUMED
   000032 00C000000000                   27+              DC     0D'0'
   000038                                28+OUTPRT         DC     X'000080000000' RES. COUNT, COM. BYTES, STATUS BYTES 3-9
   000038 00C080000000
   00003E 00                             29+              DC     AL1(0) LOGICAL UNIT CLASS
   00003F 03                             30+              DC     AL1(3) LOGICAL UNIT
   000040 00C00060                       31+              DC     A(*+32) CCW  ADDR.
   000044 00000000                       32+              DC     4X'00' CCB-ST BYTE,CSW CCW ADDRESS
   000048 00                             33+              DC     AL1(0) 3-9
   000049 00C000                         34+              DC     VL3(IJDFZZZZ) ADDR OF LOGIC MODUL3-8
   00004C 08                             35+              DC     X'08' DTF TYPE  (PRINTER)
   00004D 10                             36+              DC     AL1(16) SWITCHES
   00004E 09                             37+              DC     X'09' NORMAL  COMM. CODE
   00004F 09                             38+              DC     X'09' CONTROL COMM. CODE
   000050 00C0EB22                       39+              DC     A(PRTOUT+0) ADDRESS OF DATA IN IOAREA1
   000054 00000000                       40+              DC     4X'00' BUCKET                          3-5
   000058 0700                           41+           NOPR   0 PUT LENGTH IN REG12 (ONLY UNDEF.
   00005A 47C0 0000              00000   42+           NOP    0 LOAD USER POINTER REG
   00005E 0CC0                           43+              DC     2X'00' NOT USED                         3-5
   000060 09C0EB220000084                44+           CCW    9,PRTOUT+0,X'20',132-0
   000068                                45+IJJZ0002  EQU    *
                                       →46 *                              HOUSEKEEPING SECTION                100
  (000068) 05B0                        →47 BEGIN         BALR   11,0                                           110
   00006A                              →48               USING  *,11                                           120
```

12

```
LOC      OBJECT CODE     ADDR1 ADDR2  STMT    SOURCE STATEMENT                                          FDOS CL3-9 11/09/73

                                    → 49              OPEN     INCARD,OUTPRT                                          130
                                      50+** 360N-CL-453 OPEN         CHANGE LEVEL 3-3                     3-3
00006A 07C0                           51+             CNOP     0,4
00006C                                52+             DC       0F'0'
00006C 0000 0000         00000        53+             LA       1,=C'$$BOPEN '
       *** ERROR ***
000070 45C0 B012         0007C        54+IJJ00003 BAL          0,*+4+4*(3-1)
000074 00C00000                       55+             DC       A(INCARD)
       *** ERROR ***
000078 0CC00038                       56+             DC       A(OUTPRT)
00007C 0A02                           57+             SVC      2
                                    → 58 *                                    PROCEDURE SECTION           140
                                    → 59              GET      INCARD            (NOTE THE NAME.)         150
                                      60+** 360N-CL-453 GET          CHANGE LEVEL 3-0
00007E 0000 0000         00000        61+             L        1,=A(INCARD) GET DTF TABLE ADDRESS
       *** ERROR ***
000082 58F1 0010         00010        62+             L        15,16(1) GET LOGIC MODULE ADDRESS
000086 45EF 0008         00008        63+             BAL      14,8(15) BRANCH TO GET ROUTINE
                                    → 64              CONTROL  OUTPRT,SK,1                                162
       *** ERROR ***
                                    → 65              CNTRL    OUTPRT,SKIP,1                              151
                                      66+** 360N-CL-453 CNTRL        CHANGE LEVEL 3-9                     3-9
00008A 0000 0000         00000        67+             L        1,=A(OUTPRT) GET DTF TABLE ADDRESS
       *** ERROR ***
                                      68                       0,INVALID SECOND PARAMETER
00008E 41C0 0000         00000        69+             LA       0,0 GET OPERATION CODE
000092 58F1 0010         00010        70+             L        15,16(1) GET LOGIC MODULE ADDRESS
000096 05EF                           71+             BALR     14,15 BRANCH TO CNTRL ROUTINE
                                    → 72              PIT      OUTPRT                                     160
       *** ERROR ***
                                    → 73              PUT      OUTPRT                                     160
                                      74+** 360N-CL-453 PUT          CHANGE LEVEL 3-5                     3-5
000098 0CC0 0000         00000        75+             L        1,=A(OUTPRT) GET DTF TABLE ADDRESS
       *** ERROR ***
00009C 58F1 0010         00010        76+             L        15,16(1) GET LOGIC MODULE ADDRESS   3-5
0000A0 45EF 000C         0000C        77+             BAL      14,12(15) BRANCH TO PUT ROUTINE     3-5
                                    → 78 FINISH       CLOSE    INCARD,OUTPRT         (NOTE 'FINISH' FOR 'FINIS'.)  170
                                      79+** 360N-CL-453 CLOSE        CHANGE LEVEL 3-3                     3-3
0000A4                                80+             CNOP     0,4
0000A4                                81+FINISH       DC       0F'0'
0000A4 0000 0000         00000        82+             LA       1,=C'$$BCLOSE'
       *** ERROR ***
0000A8 45C0 B04A         000B4        83+IJJC0007 BAL          0,*+4+4*(3-1)
0000AC 00C00000                       84+             DC       A(INCARD)
       *** ERROR ***
0000B0 0CC00038                       85+             DC       A(OUTPRT)
0000B4 0A02                           86+             SVC      2
                                    → 87              EOJ                                                 180
                                      88+** 360N-CL-453 EOJ          CHANGE LEVEL 3-0
0000B6 0A0E                           89+             SVC      14
                                    → 90 *                                    AREA   DESIGNATIONS         190
```

```
         LOC  OBJECT CODE      ADDR1 ADDR2  STMT   SOURCE STATEMENT                                    FDOS CL3-9 11/09/73

        000088                        → 91 CARD     DS    0CL80                                        200
                                      → 92 A        DS    ML10                                         210
              *** ERROR ***
        000088                        → 93 B        DS    ZL10                                         220
        0000C2                        → 94          DS    CL60000                                      230
        00EB22                        → 95 PRTOUT   DS    0CL132                                       240
        00EB22 4040404040404040       → 96 5EY      DC    9C' '                                        250
              *** ERROR ***
                                      → 97          DC    CL30                                         251
              *** ERROR ***
        00EB2B C1                     → 98          DC    C'A'                                         260
        00EB2C 4040404040404040       → 99          DC    10C' '                                       270
        00EB36                        → 100 AOUT    DS    ZL9    (THIS ERROR IS NOT PICKED UP AT ALL.) 280
        00EB3F 4040404040404040       → 101         DC    10C' '                                       290
        00EB49 C2                     → 102         DC    C'B'                                         300
                                      → 103         DC    10C' '                                       310
              *** ERROR ***
        00EB4A                        → 104 BOUT    DS    ZL10                                         320
        00EB54 4040404040404040       → 105         DC    72C' '                                       330
        000068                        → 106         END   BEGIN                                        340
        00EBA0 5B5BC2D6D7C5D540         107               =C'$$BOPEN '
        00EBA8 5B5BC2C3D3D6E2C5         108               =C'$$BCLOSE'
        00EBB0 00C00000                 109               =A(INCARD)
              *** ERROR ***
        00EBB4 00C00038                 110               =A(OUTPRT)
```

```
SYMBOL     LEN   VALUE  DEFN    REFERENCES
A          C0001 0000B8 00092
AOUT       00009 00EB36 00100
B          C0010 0000B8 00093
BEGIN      C0002 000068 00047   0106
BOUT       C0010 00EB4A 00104
CARD       C0080 0000B8 00091   0017  0019
FINIS      ****UNDEFINED*****   0018
FINISH     C0004 00C0A4 C0081
IJCX0001   C0008 00C020 00019   0009
IJJC0007   C0004 0000A8 00083
IJJ00003   C0004 000070 00054
IJJZ0001   C0001 000032 00023
IJJZ0002   C0001 000068 00045
INCARD     ****UNDEFINED*****   0055  0061  0084  0109
INCARDS    C0006 000000 00006
O          ****UNDEFINED*****   0001
OUTPRT     C0006 00C038 00028   0056  0067  0075  0085  0110
PRTOUT     00132 00E822 00095   0039  0044
TWO        C0001 000000 00001
```

```
                              DIAGNOSTICS                                PAGE    1

STMT   ERROR CODE    MESSAGE                                             11/09/73

   1   IJY025        NEAR OPERAND COLUMN    1--RELOCATABILITY ERROR
  18   IJY024        NEAR OPERAND COLUMN    3--UNDEFINED SYMBOL
  26   IJY037        MNOTE STATEMENT
  53   IJY035        NEAR OPERAND COLUMN   15--ADDRESSABILITY ERROR
  55   IJY024        NEAR OPERAND COLUMN    3--UNDEFINED SYMBOL
  61   IJY035        NEAR OPERAND COLUMN   13--ADDRESSABILITY ERROR
  64   IJY088        UNDEFINED OPERATION CODE
  67   IJY035        NEAR OPERAND COLUMN   13--ADDRESSABILITY ERROR
  68   IJY037        MNOTE STATEMENT
  72   IJY088        UNDEFINED OPERATION CODE
  75   IJY035        NEAR OPERAND COLUMN   13--ADDRESSABILITY ERROR
  82   IJY035        NEAR OPERAND COLUMN   15--ADDRESSABILITY ERROR
  84   IJY024        NEAR OPERAND COLUMN    3--UNDEFINED SYMBOL
  92   IJY031        NEAR OPERAND COLUMN    1--UNKNOWN TYPE
  96   IJY016        INVALID NAME
  97   IJY107        NEAR OPERAND COLUMN    5--INVALID OPERAND
 103   IJY031        NEAR OPERAND COLUMN    2--UNKNOWN TYPE
 109   IJY024        NEAR OPERAND COLUMN    4--UNDEFINED SYMBOL


 18 STATEMENTS FLAGGED IN THIS ASSEMBLY
```

```
OP77I JOB TWO         CANCELED DUE TO INVALID ADDRESS
OS07I PROBLEM PROGRAM PSW      FF050001 00027BA
                                       ↑       ↑
                                       |       Instruction
                                       |       Address
                                       Interruption
                                       Code
```

```
        TWO           11/09/73                                                   12.02.52              PAGE   1

   GR 0-7   0C000000  00002800  0000FFFF  00002800    0000FF84  FFFFFF7C  00000000  000027B8
   GR 8-F   0C00430A  0A0107F1  00002810  00002810    000037D8  000047D8  00000288  0000007B
   FP REG   42F00000  00000000  42F00000  00000000    BEBB9000  00000000  00000000  00000000
   COMREG   BG ADDR IS 000288

   000000   0C000000  00000000  00000000  00000000    00000000  00000288  FF050000  00000000    ....  ....  ....  ....    ....  ....  ....  ....
   000020   FF070007  40002386  00000000  00000000    5B5BC2C5  D6D1F440  FF05000E  80002386    ....  . ..  ....  ....    $$BEOJ4 .  ....  . ..
   000040   0C0024A8  08000000  00002498  00000000    FCE38300  01C3701B  00C40000  0F00151E    ....  ....  ....  ....    ..T.  . ..  ....  ....
   000060   0C040000  C0000450  00040000  000014E2    00000000  000040A8C  00040000  00C0035C    ....  ....  ....  ....    ....  ....  ....  ..*.
   000080   0C000000  00000000  00040000  00000003    000506B0  06B006B0  41BB0073  4570010E    ....  ....  ....  ....    ....  ....  ....  ....
   0000A0   940FB4E3  41A0BA40  4190013E  4180B3C6    47F000D2  06B006B0  06B006B0  06B006B0    ..T.  ...  ....  ....    .... ....  ....  ....
   0000C0   06B041BB  C01741BB  000504570  010E4180   013E9640  A0019120  A00C4710  00EA9265    .... ....  ....  ....     ....  ....  ....  ....
   0000E0   A00195E2  A0024780  0CDC9510  02F70778    94F902C3  D70102E0  02E09680  BA414400    ....&. ..  ....  .. .     ....  ....  ....  ....
   000100   B2C60788  947FBA41  4570B360  07F842B0    00DF5880  02109180  A0000717  5890A0C4    .F..  ....  ....  ....     ....  ....  ..-.  -.8.
   000120   488001D2  5000902C  D21B9010  01F0D207    00800900  9680A0C0  07F74570  0116D203    ...K&.  ..K.  ....  .OK.    ....  ....  ....  .9.CP
   000140   0FA60FAA  58E0021C  DC030FA6  BA301BAA    DD030FA6  000C43A1  000442A0  02B741AA    ....  ....  ....  ....     ....  ....  ..7.  ..K.
   000160   BA30D200  043102B7  95200431  47400186    95600431  47800180  92400431  47F00186    ..K.  ....  ....  ....    ....  ....  ....  ....
   000180   D2000431  04304590  02224400  A0045890    A0044220  AC009140  A0014710  B92AD207    K...  ....  ....  ....    ....  ....  ....  ..K.
   0001A0   01F09008  98989010  820001F0  45900222    956002B7  478001D4  5890A004  98189030    ....  ....  ....  ....    ....  ....  ..0.  ....
   0001C0   91020021  478001CC  92000432  989F01F0    82000038  9284BA90  47F001C0  9680A0C0    ....  ....  ....  ....    ....  ....  ....  -...M...
   0001E0   41100030  47F0B2C6  615C4061  504044F0    000027A8  00001A40  00000288  00000000    ....  ....  ....  ....    ....  ....  ....  0...
   000200   8C0021CC  A000227E  000020D0  90001188    00001000  00002000  00003C00  00000000    ....  .. .  O.F/*  /& .O   ....  ....  ....  ....
   000220   1AA8D500  04310432  07899068  04185880    00505980  0F9C47D0  02428A80  000847F0    .N..  ....  ....  ....    ....  ....  ....  ..O.
   000240   02468880  C0085F80  00541078  5E700434    50800434  95400432  47400274  5880043C    ....  ....  ....  ....    ....  ....  ....  ....
   000260   5E708020  5C708020  D2000432  04319868    041807F9  5880043C  5E70801C  5070801C    ..&..K..  ....  ....  ....  &.  ....  .9.&....
   000280   47F00268  C0000000  F1F161F0  F961F7E3    28002800  00000000  00000000  00000000    ..E..K..  .  11/09/73    ....  .9.E.  ....   The date with /.
   0002A0   E3E6D640  40404040  0000FFFF  00004E4B    00011447  00000010  0000FFFF  68204E90     TWO  Name of the program.                     The date.
   0002C0   28A04ED0  C0AF1849  1B501BA1  1BA21BF4    1CD01CD4  1CD838F1  F1F0F9F7  F3F3F1F3    ....  ....  ....  ....    ....  ....  ...  .M.Q. 110973 B13
   0002E0   0C001A30  C0000000E  0F180F3A  0FA80FB0    0FB80010  1B2C0010  5B5BC2D6  00130008    ....  ....  ....  ....4    ....  ....  $$BO....
   000300   02000FEC  1A2C0000  00000000  02881080    00000314  00000000  00000000  00000004    ....  ....  ....  ....    ....  ....  ....  ....
   000320   0C000FC0  C0000000  00000000  00000000    00000000  00000000  00000000  00000000    ....  ....  ....  ....    ....  ....  ....  ....
   000340   0C000000  C0000000  00000418  00001D50    00001AA0  00000EE0  00001DE4  923801D3    ....  ....  ....  ....    ....  ....  ....E  ....
   000360   909F01F0  98BE0210  41900818  98BE0210    90690418  4590039C  98690418  951002B7    .0..  ....  ....  ....    ....  ....  ....U.  .L
   000380   47700392  58A0BA44  9018A030  41A0BA40    07F941A0  BA909601  A00007F9  D2C00431    ....  ....  ....  ....    ....  ....  .9..  .9K.
   0003A0   04325880  C0505980  0F9C47D0  03B68A80    000847F0  03BA8880  00085F80  00541078    ....  ....  ....  ....    ....  ....  .0..  ....
   0003C0   5E700434  951002B7  478003D2  D2000430    04329130  04324770  03F69140  04320719    ....  ....  KK..  ....    ....  ....  ....  .6. ..
   0003E0   50800434  5880043C  5E708024  50708024    92400432  07F99528  01D30789  50800434    ....  ....  ....  ....    ....  &...  ..9.  L.&.
   000400   5880043C  5E70801C  5070801C  952001D3    07899240  043207F9  0C0008A2  80C00802    ....  &...  ....  L..    ....  ....  9...  ....
   000420   0C000734  00000818  00000000  00C00001    10000000  FF396FB7  00001DC8  00001D50    ....  ....  ....  ....    ....  ....  ....  H..&
   000440   0C000000  C0000000  00000000  0000001C    909F01F0  922001D3  4590036C  419001AC    ....  ....  ....  ....    .0..  ....  ....  .L..
   000460   95C00023  478004F0  95260023  478000B6    48600022  1A664870  02204866  7CC007F6    ....  ....  ....  ....    .0..  L..  ....  ...6
   000480   181F4860  0F481833  18234320  1007950B    10074780  04BC47F0  053A4720  00C21823    ....  ....  ....  ....    .-..  ....  ....  ...6
   0004A0   950B1007  478C04B0  950B1007  47F00536    4330BA3A  47F00546  472000C0  96801002    ....  ....  ....  ....    .0..  ....  0...  .B..
   0004C0   960C1004  07F91858  41430002  43540000    41455000  1A444A40  0F4095FF  40004770    ....  ....  ....  ....    .9..  ....  0...  ....
   0004E0   04CC4284  C0007F9   95FF0567  07891B00    95FF0567  47808372  92400432  956002B7    ....  ....  ....  ....    .&.  ....  ....  ....
   000500   47800480  41600010  D502A005  03014770    05204111  00004910  0E6047B0  05201B66    ....  ....  ....  ....    .9..  ....  .N..  ....
   000520   1B334330  10079501  10064770  049A4123    00B950F  100747B0  00C24182  2C004870    ....  ....  ....  ....    ....  ....  ....  ....
   000540   02D44338  7000D403  1002BA9C  49300E5E    47B004B8  89300003  4133BB50  91F03004    ....  ....  ....  ....    ....  ....  .B..  ....
   000560   4780B654  418C0002  41488000  1A444A40    0F404158  BB2CD200  05674C00  50104000    .M..  .M..  ....  ....    ....  ....  ....  .&.O.
   000580   92FF4000  04324500  4260500E  91F03004    4780B674  47F0059C  58800FE4  44000B88    ....  &..&..O.   ....  ....  ....K..  ....  .U..
   0005A0   9560BA88  47700616  D2020355  10095860    03594507  60004770  0616D202  03556001    ....  ....  ....  ....    ....  ....  ....  ....
   0005C0   58700354  1B444340  30054C40  0F365A40    03584144  00000503  70014C00  47800616    ....  ....  ..K.  .-..    ....  .K.  -....K..-.
   0005E0   9120100C  4710C610  91051002  47700610    91406004  47800610  94BF6004  91101002    ....  ..).  ....  ....    ....  .N..  ....  ....
```

```
              TWO             11/09/73                                                                                   PAGE   5

001A40  0310C2C7 19000FEC 0C002800 240B0F80   0000B300 000000C0 000000E0 FF0060C0   ..BG............   ........-.......
001A60  CC000000 13000802 5B5BC2C1 E3E3D5C1   8000C1D9 47F00E26 000027A8 07C020D0   ........$$BATTNA   ....AR.O........
001A80  84006150 47F00CAA 0000000E 00001B60   8400E2D7 47F001D4 1B700016 1F05C0C0   ../&.O.........-   ....SP.M........
001AA0  CC000000 00000000 00001292 12C61386   13EA13CE 00BA1404 14301424 14D01348   ................   ......F.........
001AC0  14501464 C0C604E8 161815EE 161415EA   161815EE 01AC00B6 147800B6 01AC00B6   .E...F.Y........   ................
001AE0  C0B600B6 C0B600B6 00B601AC 01AC00B6   00B618FC 030028B8 00002488 01002488   ................   ................
001B00  04000000 05000000 06000000 07000000   08000000 09CCCCC0 0A000C00 0BC0C000   ................   ................
001B20  0C00C000 0D000000 FF00C000 0D030300   00000000 000C0000 0000FFFF FFFFFFFF   ................   ................
001B40  FFFFFFFF FFFFFFFF 000004FF FFFFFFFF   000CFF00 110000FC 001FFF00 00C000F8   ................   ...............8
001B60  CC0EFF00 40C080FC 000DFF00 21C000FC   0190FF00 600000FC 0191FF00 600100FC   ................   -.-.8....-......
001B80  0192FF00 600200F8 0180FF00 50C300C0   0181FF01 50C300C0 FF000000 0C000000   .-..8....&C.....   .&C.............
001BA0  FF01B3B7 28FF0000 00020000 00030000   00040000 00050000 00060000 00070000   ................   ................
001BC0  0C080000 0C090C00 00A0000 00B0000     000C0000 000D0000 000E0000 000F0000   ................   ................
001BE0  CC100000 00110000 00120000 00130000   00FF0002 00000000 00000000 00000000   ................   ........* PROGRA
001C00  09001C18 2000002B 00008000 0CC00004   00001C00 00001C08 5C40D7D9 D6C7D9C1   ................   M TO ILLUSTRATE    SOME ERROR MESSA
001C20  D440E3D6 40C9D3D3 E4E2E3D9 C1E3C540   E2D6D4C5 40C5D9D9 D6D940D4 C5E2E2C1   ................   GES.............
001C40  C7C5E200 00000000 00000000 00000000   00000000 00000000 00000000 00000000   ................   ................
001C60  CC000000 C0000000 09001C80 20000033   00008000 0C000004 00001C68 00001C70   ................   OP77I JOB TWO      CANCELED DUE
001C80  F0D7F7F7 C940D1D6 C240E3E6 D6404040   404040C3 C1D5C3C5 D3C5C440 C4E4C540   ................   TO INVALID ADDRE SS
001CA0  E3D640C9 D5E5C1D3 C9C440C1 C4C4D9C5   E2E24000 00000000 00000000 00000000   ................   ................
001CC0  00000000 00C00000 00000000 00000000   000BFFFF 0B0F0C00 00FF00FF 03FF02FF   ................   ................
001CE0  01FF0400 04FFFFFF FFFF01FF FFFFFFFF   04FF05FF 05FF04FF FFFFFFFF FFFFFFFF   ................   ................
001D00  FFFFFFFF FFFFFFFF FFFFFFFF 00000000   00000000 00000000 00000000 00000000   ................   ....
001D20  CC000000 --SAME--                     0000F1F2 F0F0F4F3 00000000 01000000   ................   .120043.........
001D40  0C000000 C0000000 00000000 0CC00000   00000456 00001C2F E3E6D640 40404040   ................   ........TWO
001D60  19000000 00000000 00000000 00C00168   40404040 40404040 C2C725E2 F1F161F0   ................   ........BG.S11/0
001D80  E3E6D640 40404040 40404040 40404040   40404040 40404040 00011447 00000000   TWO                9/73............
001DA0  F961F7F3 0120043F 0000000F 00C00000   40404040 40404040 00011447 00000000   ................   ................
001DC0  CC000000 00000000 00000000 00001E05   00006DD3 00B00000 00B20009 00000000   ................   ...L............
001DE0  00000000 00001300 000000C7 00000000   0000 00FF 00000000 00000000 00000000   .......G........   ....
001E00  CC000000 --SAME--
0020C0  CC000000 00000000 00000000 00000000

        LBLTYP   HEX LENGTH IS 0000
        --BG--
0027A0                             D5D640D5 C1D4C540   FF050001 400027BA 0A0107F1 00002810                      NO NAME   .... .......1....
0027C0  0C002810 C00037D8 000047D8 00000288   0000007B 00000000 00002800 0000FFFF   .......Q...Q....   ................
0027E0  0C002800 C000FF84 FFFFFF7C 00000000   000027B8 000004B0A 00000000 00C5F382   .........'......   .............E3.
002800  0C008000 00000000 00002820 00C00000   000113B8 02010202 000028B8 00000000   ................   ................
002820  020028B8 20000050 47000000 47000000   00000000 00000000 00008000 00000003   ........&.......   ................
002840  00002860 00000000 00011420 08100909   00011322 00000000 07004700 00000000   ................   ................
002860  09011322 20000084 05B00700 00000000   4500B012 00000000 00002838 0A020000   ..............BALR...........   ...............
002880  0C0058F1 C01045EF 00080000 00004100   000058F1 001005EF 00000000 58F10010   ...1............   .......1......1.
0028A0  45EF000C C0000000 4500B04A 00C00000   00002838 0A020A0E 00004C9E 00004CD6   ................   ...........)....)
0028C0  0C004D68 C0004D82 00004DBE 00004DDA   00004DF4 00004E70 F8404040 F9404040   ................   .......4...8...9
0028E0  C1404040 C2404040 C3404040 C4404040   C5404040 C6404040 E7404040 40404040   A       B       C       D           E       F       X
002900  98EFE008 47F0F100 40404040 40404040   40404040 40404040 40404040 07FE05F0   .....01.           ...0
002920  983BF054 58C0F014 58E0F034 07FE0029   1E002868 00404040 40404040 40404094   ..O...O...O.....   ......              .
002940  0022006E 00740088 00260078 00000000   00000000 00000000 00000000 00000000   ................   ................
002960  0C004040 40404040 40404040 40404040   40404040 40404040 40404040 40404040   ..                 ..
002980  40404040 40404040 40404000 00000000   5B5BC2D6 D7C5D540 5B5BC2C3 D3D6E2C5   ................   $$BOPEN $$BCLOSE
0029A0  0C002800 00002838 0A320000 0A320000   47F0F01A 0A320000 C9D1C3C6 E9C9E9F0   ................   .00.....IJCFZIZO
0029C0  030A0A00 91801002 4710F026 0A0750E0   F06458E0 10209101 10044780 F04C9140   ........0...&....  0............O).
0029E0  10024710 F04658E0 F06447F0 F01A58E0   101C07FE D501F060 E0004770 F05A47F0   ........0..00...   ....N.O-....0...0
```

Program Three

Adding Three Numbers (Binary)

Even though computers work very fast, they don't think at all. People don't work as fast, but they think quickly. In most cases, human thoughts are not easy to follow step-by-step because the mind seems to skip instantaneously from one step to another which is, perhaps, a hundred steps away.

This is the difficulty in programming a computer. In the program that follows, the problem was a simple one: to read three numbers (one on each of three cards), add them, and print a sentence. The trouble is that the programmer cannot tell the computer to go ahead and add the three numbers. He has to tell the computer *step by step* what is to be done. At this point, the programmer has to slow his thoughts down to practically snail's pace to avoid skipping anything.

The programmer must visualize exactly what is happening. The steps are somewhat as follows:

1. The numbers are punched on cards. (Where exactly are the numbers? In what form are the numbers?)
2. The cards are stacked in the card reader, right after the // EXEC card. In this case there are three of them. There is a /* card after the three data cards.
3. The computer reads *one* card. (Where shall it go? In what form does it exist at this moment?)
4. The computer reads a second card. No, that can't be right. The second card would read right on top of the first card. Then, instead, *move* the first number out so that the second number won't destroy it upon being input into the very same memory locations.
5. Now the computer can read the second card. The first card image is destroyed, but that doesn't matter any more since the first number has been saved.
6. Move the second number away to a safe place.
7. Read the third card. As mentioned, the second card image is destroyed, but that no longer matters.
8. Move the third number. (Is this really necessary?)
9. The three numbers are in zoned form, because any number read in on a card is in zoned form. For example, 463 reads in as F4F6F3. Arithmetic cannot be done in zoned form. This program deals with *binary* addition, so the numbers must be converted to binary. But wait, zoned numbers don't convert directly to binary. First, they must be converted to packed form. The zoned number, F4F6F3, must become 463C or 463F, which are equivalent.
10. Now, convert from packed to binary.
11. The result of X is that the three numbers, in binary form, are in three different registers. There are several ways of proceeding, but the registers can be added, in pairs.
12. Now the sum, in binary form, is in a register. In order to print it, it must be in zoned form, but there is no way to go directly from binary to zoned. The sum is first converted to packed form.

13. The packed form is converted to zoned form ("unpacked").
14. Now the sentence must be printed. If everything is in the right place, a PUT will print a single line.

The next column shows, in diagram form, the *flowchart* for steps 1 through 14. In practice, as programmers gain experience, they tend to omit (in the flowchart only) some of the obvious steps, but the beginner does well to make rather detailed flowcharts.

In the program which follows the flowchart, note the following:

1. Statement 28. The option: CONTROL=YES has been added to the DTFPR. Statement 98 can now be used to have the printer skip to the top of the next page. In this way, the result of the program is printed on a fresh page instead of immediately following the // EXEC.
2. Three GET instructions were required for the three cards. This is not a good method (suppose there were 10,000 cards!). It will do for this beginning program.
3. In the answer, page 22, the number -57 is printed as 5P, and the number 443 was printed as 44C. The reason is that -57 was unpacked into F5D7, and D7 is the same as P. Also, 443 was unpacked as F4F4C3, and C3 is the same as C. (In both bases, verify by looking at your green card.) What is needed is *editing*, to be done in two later programs. This is just a beginning.
4. The print line is set up in statements 126 through 136. It requires study.

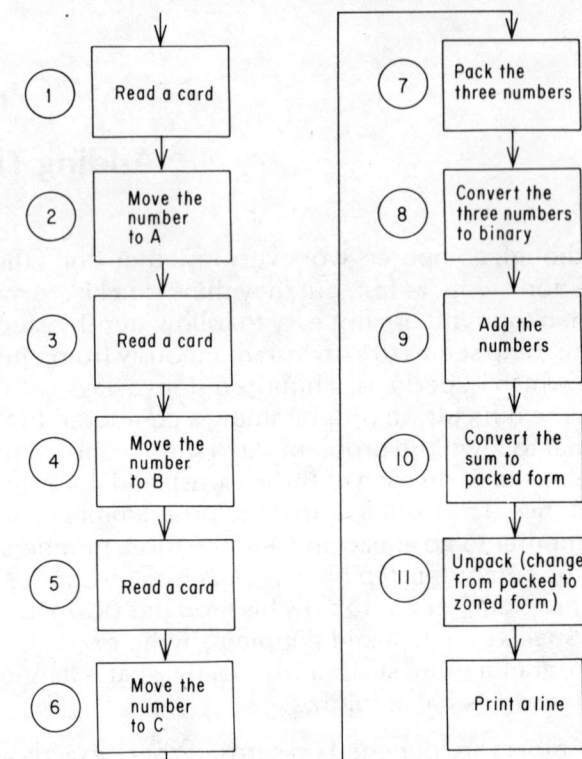

Assembly Language Basics

```
// JOB THREE                              12.19.42
* ADDING THREE NUMBERS.
// OPTION LINK                                030
// EXEC ASSEMBLY                              040


  LOC  OBJECT CODE      ADDR1 ADDR2  STMT   SOURCE STATEMENT                                    FDCS CL3-9 11/09/73
                                       1  * THE INPUT WAS THREE CARDS WITH 463, 37, AND
                                       2  * -57 RIGHT-ADJUSTED IN CC 1 - 10.  REMEMBER THAT -57
                                       3  * IS PUNCHED WITH A 5 IN CC 9 AND A DOUBLE-PUNCHED 7 IN CC 10.
                                       4            PRINT NOGEN
000000                                 5  THREE     START
                                       6  *                              DTF SECTION
                                       7  CARDF     DTFCD DEVADDR=SYSRDR,IOAREA1=IMAGE,EOFADDR=END        sets up an IBM-
                                      28  PRINTF    DTFPR DEVADDR=SYSLST,IOAREA1=OUTPUT,BLKSIZE=132,CONTROL=YES   supplied program
                                      49  *                              HOUSEKEEPING                             allowing control
000068 05B0                           50  HOYSEE    BALR  11,0                                                    over the printer.
00006A                                51            USING *,11
                                      52            OPEN  CARDF,PRINTF
                                      61  *                              PROCEDURE SECTION
                                      62            GET   CARDF
00008A D209 B122 B0A6  0018C 00110    67            MVC   A,X
                                      68  *                              The # blank card was inserted to make the listing easier to read.
                                      69            GET   CARDF
00009C D209 B131 B0A6  0019B 00110    74            MVC   B,X
                                      75  *
                                      76            GET   CARDF
0000AE D209 B140 B0A6  001AA 00110    81            MVC   C,X
                                      82  *                              PACK THE NUMBERS           It is always a good
0000B4 F279 B17E B122  001E8 0018C    83            PACK  PKA,A                                     idea to include as much
0000BA F279 B186 B131  001F0 0019B    84            PACK  PKB,B                                     explanation as possible.
0000C0 F279 B18E B140  001F8 001AA    85            PACK  PKC,C
                                      86  *                              CONVERT TO BINARY
0000C6 4F30 B17E       001E8          87            CVB   3,PKA
0000CA 4F40 B186       001F0          88            CVB   4,PKB
0000CE 4F60 B18E       001F8          89            CVB   6,PKC
                                      90  *                              ADD
0000D2 1A43                           91            AR    4,3    A+B IN R4            Comments are useful for individual instructions as well.
0000D4 1A64                           92            AR    6,4    A+B+C IN R6
                                      93  *                              CONVERT TO DECIMAL
0000D6 4E60 B196       00200          94            CVD   6,SUMP   PACKED SUM IN SUMP
                                      95  *                              PREPARE FOR PRINTING
0000DA F397 B14E B196  001B8 00200    96            UNPK  SUM,SUMP TAKES PACKED # IN SUMP,AND PLACES RESULT IN SUM
                                      97  *                              OUTPUT
                                      98            CNTRL PRINTF,SK,1      SKIP TO TOP OF PAGE
                                     104            PUT   PRINTF
                                     109  *                              ENDING THE PROGRAM
                                     110  END       CLOSE CARDF,PRINTF
                                     119            EOJ
                                     122  *                              AREA DEFINITIONS
                                     123  IMAGE     DS    0CL80
000110                               124  X         DS    ZL10                        can be used if the
000110                               125            DS    CL70                        DTFPR has
00011A                               126  OUTPUT    DS    0CL132                      CONTROL=YES
000160                               127            DC    CL33' '
000160 404040404040404040            128            DC    CL11' THE SUM OF '
000181 40E3C8C540E2E4D4              129  A         DS    ZL10
00018C                               130            DC    CL5' AND '
000196 40C1D5C440
```

Because of the 0 in 0CL80, IMAGE and X are at the same location.

These are blanks. The printout shows but a few.

```
         LOC  OBJECT CODE        ADDR1 ADDR2  STMT    SOURCE STATEMENT

        00019B                                131 B       DS    ZL10
        0001A5  40C1D5C440                    132         DC    CL5' AND '
        0001AA                                133 C       DS    ZL10
        0001B4  40C9E240                      134         DC    CL4' IS '
        0001B8                                135 SUM     DS    ZL10
        0001C2  4040404040404040              136         DC    CL34' '
        0001E8                                137 PKA     DS    D
        0001F0                                138 PKB     DS    D
        0001F8                                139 PKC     DS    D
        000200                                140 SUMP    DS    D
        000068                                141         END   HOYSEE
        000208  5B5BC2D6D7C5D540              142               =C'$$BOPEN '
        000210  5B5BC2C3D3D6E2C5              143               =C'$$BCLOSE'
        000218  0CCC0000                      144               =A(CARDF)
        00021C  0CCC0038                      145               =A(PRINTF)
```

THE SUM OF   463 AND   37 AND   5P IS 000000044C   } ANSWER

Program Four

Snapshot Method (Partial Dumps)

In this program, two numbers defined within the program (statements 116 and 118) are packed, then changed to binary. They are added. Then the sum is converted to packed form and unpacked, but not edited. The purpose of this program is to trace the procedure by a series of "snapshots." In this method, the instruction

PDUMP FIRST,SECOND

will (1) display the contents of all the registers and (2) dump everything from FIRST up to but *not including* SECOND.

For demonstration purposes, all the registers from GPR 0 to GPR 15 (16 registers) were filled with blanks *except for the base register*, in this case register 11. This was done in statement 40. (Reminder: All the instructions are explained and illustrated in the Appendix.)

It is of great value to follow the program by means of the dumps. Dumps 2 and 3 will be explained as a starter, leaving the other dumps for the reader's practice.

Statement 50 is an instruction which requires the computer to dump the registers and all the areas from A up to BLANKS. Looking at the area definitions, this means that the following have been requested:

LOC	LABEL	CONTENT
0EC	A	zoned 4345
0F4	B	zoned -3765
0FC	PK	A (packed)

Turning to the second dump on page 27, note that registers 0, 1, 3, and 11 have things in them. What are they?

Register 0 has an address 29E8. At this installation, the relocation factor for this type of program is 2800_x. Subtracting, the location is $29E8_x - 2800_x = 1E8_x$. When we look at that location, statement 140 shows that this is the *address constant* for the operand of the PDUMP instruction.

Register 1 has the address 29D8. This translates into location 1D8 which is statement 138. At this position, the computer has stored an *entry point value* for the PDUMP subroutine.

Register 3 has a $10F9_x$ which is 4345_{10}. The calculation is:

$$1 * 16^3 = 4{,}096$$
$$0 * 16^2 = 0$$
$$15 * 16^1 = 240$$
$$9 * 16^0 = 9$$

which adds up to 4345_{10}. In other words, the $10F9_x$ register 3 is correct.

Register 11 has the address 2832_x. By this time, the reader recognizes this as equivalent to the location 32_x. In the program, this is the location at the USING (statement 31). To clarify the base-displacement method again, look at statement 48. This has two operands: DOUBLE and PK. For explanatory purposes, concentrate on PK. In statement 120, the location of PK is 0000FC. Checking with the left side of statement 48, 000FC is under ADDR2 as expected. So far, so good. The USING is at 000032. Subtracting 32_x from FC_x, the *displacement* is $0CA_x$. Because the base register is B_x (= 11 in decimal), the base-displacement address should be B0CA. So it is.

A is at location 0000EC according to statement 116. To find it in the dump, add the relocation factor, 2800_x. The resulting address is $28EC_x$. In the dump, note that the computer has 0028E0 at the beginning of the line. This is the address of the first byte of the line. Remembering that *two* hex characters are equal to 1 byte, each group of 8 characters is a fullword (4 bytes). The 8 fullwords for this line of print are at: 28E0, 28E4, 28E8, 28EC, 28F0, 28F4, 28F8, and 28FC, all in hex. The number

F4F3F4C5

is at 28EC, the correct spot for A.
All the other numbers should be found for practice.

In dump 3 (statement 57), the computer was instructed to dump from PK *up to but not including* PK. Therefore, PK was not dumped at all. However, the registers were dumped. Register 0 has 29F0x which (after subtracting 2800x for this installation) is equivalent to location 1F0x. At this location, statement 141 has the address constant for the operand of the PDUMP instruction.

Notice that the computer uses registers for its own purposes. It is wise to avoid registers 0,1,2,13,14,15 unless they are really needed urgently, because the computer uses these from time to time. Register 2 is usually safe if you really need it.

```
// JOB FOUR                              12.21.50
*  SNAPSHOT METHOD                                        02C
// OPTION LINK                                            03C
// EXEC ASSEMBLY

   LOC    OBJECT CODE   ADDR1 ADDR2  STMT   SOURCE STATEMENT                                FDOS CL3-9 11/09/73

                                        1 * IN THIS PROGRAM, THE 'PDUMP' IS USED TO PROVIDE A 'SNAPSHOT' OF THE      040
                                        2 * GENERAL PURPOSE AND FLOATING POINT REGISTERS AND SELECTED AREAS OF       050
                                        3 * CORE. NOTICE THAT THESE AREAS HAVE BEEN PLACED ON FULLWORD BOUNDARIES    060
                                        4 * TO FACILITATE DEBUGGING.                                                 070
                                        5         PRINT  NOGEN                                                       080
   000000                               6 FOUR    START                                                              090
                                        7 *                      DTF SECTION                                         100
                                        8 PRINTF  DTFPR BLKSIZE=132,DEVADDR=SYSLST,IOAREA1=PRINT,CONTROL=YES          120
                                       29 *                      HOUSEKEEPING SECTION                                140
   000030 05B0                         30 BEGIN   BALR   11,0                                                        150
   000032                              31         USING  *,11                                                        160
                                       32         OPEN   PRINTF                                                      170
   000042 98CA B00A             0010C  40         LM     12,10,BLANKS    CLEARS ALL GPR EXCEPT GPR 11                180
                                       41 *                      PROCEDURE SECTION                                   190
   000046 F223 B0CA B0BA 000FC 000EC   42         PACK   PK,A            04 34 5C                                    200
                                       43 DUMP1   PDUMP  PK,DOUBLE       DUMPS REGISTERS AND 'PK'         }#1        210
   000056 F872 B0CE B0CA 00100 000FC   48         ZAP    DOUBLE,PK                                                   220
   00005C 4F30 B0CE       00100        49         CVB    3,DOUBLE        10F9 IN GPR 3                               230
                                       50 DUMP2   PDUMP  A,BLANKS        DUMPS REGISTERS AND AREAS FROM 'A' }#2      240
                                       55 *                              TO 'SUM'                                    250
   00006A F223 B0CA B0C2 000FC 000F4   56         PACK   PK,B            03 76 5D                                    260
                                       57 DUMP3   PDUMP  PK,PK           DUMPS REGISTERS ONLY (NOT 'PK')  }#3        270
   00007A F872 B0CE B0CA 00100 000FC   62         ZAP    DOUBLE,PK                                                   280
   000080 4F40 B0CE       00100        63         CVB    4,DOUBLE        F-F14B                                      290
                                       64 DUMP4   PDUMP  PK,BLANKS       DUMPS REGISTERS AND AREAS FROM 'PK' }#4     300
                                       69 *                              TO 'SUM'                                    310
   00008E 1A34                         70         AR     3,4             BINARY A+B (0-0244) IN GPR 3                320
                                       71 DUMP5   PDUMP  SUM,BLANKS      DUMPS REGISTERS AND 'SUM'        }#5        330
   00009A 4E30 B0CE       00100        76         CVD    3,DOUBLE        00 00 00 00 00 00 58 0C                     350
   00009E F337 B0D6 B0CE 00108 00100   77         UNPK   SUM,DOUBLE      F0 F5 F8 C0                                 360
                                       78 DUMP6   PDUMP  PK,BLANKS       DUMPS REGISTERS AND AREAS FROM 'PK' }#6     370
                                       83 *                              TO 'SUM'                                    380
   0000AE D203 B12C B0BA 0015E 000EC   84         MVC    AOUT,A          F4 F3 F4 C5 = 434E (NOT EDITED)             390
   0000B4 D203 B148 B0C2 0017A 000F4   85         MVC    BOUT,B          F3 F7 F6 D5 = 376N (NOT EDITED)             400
   0000BA D203 B166 B0D6 00198 00108   86         MVC    SUMOUT,SUM      F0 F5 F8 C0 = 0580 (NOT EDITED)             410
                                       87 *                                                                          420
                                       88         CNTRL  PRINTF,SK,1     SKIP TO TOP OF PAGE                         435
                                       94         PUT    PRINTF                                                      440
                                       99         CLOSE  PRINTF                                                      450
                                      107         EOJ                                                                460
                                      110 *                      AREA DEFINITIONS                                    470
                                      111 * THE AREAS FOR DUMPING HAVE BEEN PLACED ON FULLWORD BOUNDARIES, WITH      480
                                      112 * BLANK FILLERS BETWEEN THEM. THIS CAN BE DONE EVERYWHERE EXCEPT           490
                                      113 * IN I/O AREAS. AFTER THE PROGRAM IS DEBUGGED, THE BOUNDARY                491
                                      114 * CARDS AND PDUMPS SHOULD, OF COURSE, BE REMOVED.                          493
   0000EC                             115         DS     0F              TO PROVIDE FULLWORD ALIGNMENT               500
   0000EC F4F3F4C5                    116 A       DC     ZL4'4345'                                                   510
   0000F0 40404040                    117         DC     CL4' '          FILLER   Sometimes inserted                 520
   0000F4 F3F7F6D5                    118 B       DC     ZL4'-3765'                                                  530
   0000F8 40404040                    119         DC     CL4' '          FILLER   to make the dump                   540
                                                                                  easier to read.
   0000FC                             120 PK      DS     PL3                                                         550
```

25

```
LOC      OBJECT CODE      ADDR1 ADDR2    STMT    SOURCE STATEMENT                                    FDCS CL3-9 11/09/73

000OFF   40                                121            DC     C' '              (FILLER)          560
000100                                    122    DOUBLE  DS     D                                    570
000108                                    123    SUM     DS     ZL4                                  580
00010C   4040404040404040                  124    BLANKS  DC     CL60' '                              590
000148                                    125    PRINT   DS     0CL132                               600
000148   4040404040404040                  126            DC     20C' '                               610
00015C   C17E                              127            DC     C'A='                                620
00015E                                    128    AOUT    DS     ZL4                                  630
000162   4040404040404040                  129            DC     22C' '                               640
000178   C27E                              130            DC     C'B='                                650
00017A                                    131    BOUT    DS     ZL4                                  660
00017E   4040404040404040                  132            DC     22C' '                               670
000194   C14EC27E                          133            DC     CL4'A+B='                            680
000198                                    134    SUMOUT  DS     ZL4                                  690
00019C   4040404040404040                  135            DC     48C' '                               700
000030                                    136            END    BEGIN                                710
0001D0   5B5BC2D6D7C5D540                  137                   =C'$$BOPEN '
0001D8   5B5BC2D7C4E4D4D7                  138                   =CL8'$$BPDUMP'
0001E0   0CC000FC00C00100                  139                   =A(PK,DOUBLE)
0001E8   CCC00EC00C0010C                   140                   =A(A,BLANKS)
0001F0   0CC000FC00C000FC                  141                   =A(PK,PK)
0001F8   0CC000FC00C0010C                  142                   =A(PK,BLANKS)
000200   0CC00108000010C                   143                   =A(SUM,BLANKS)
000208   5B5BC2C3D3D6E2C5                  144                   =C'$$BCLOSE'
000210   00000000                          145                   =A(PRINTF)
```

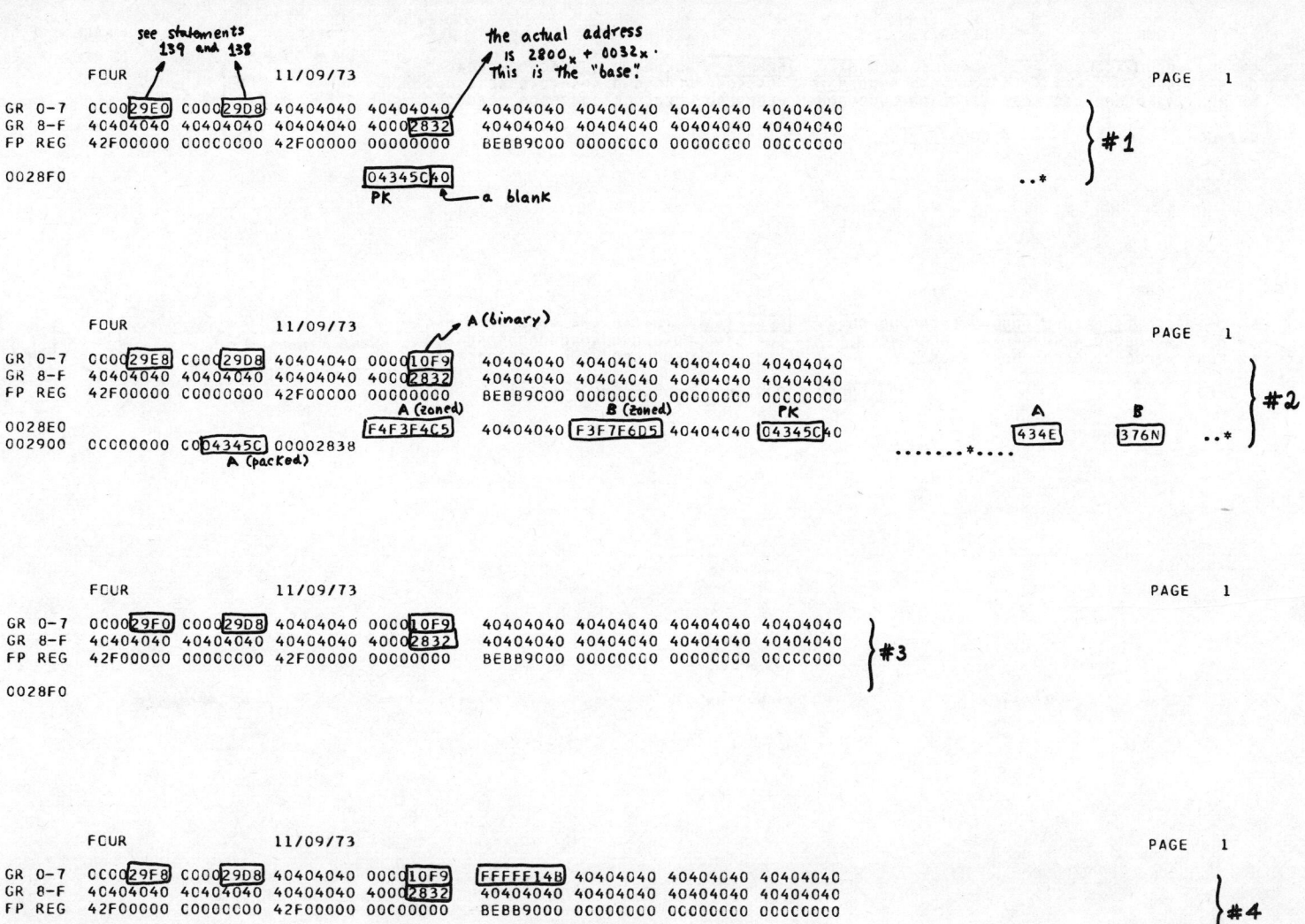

```
              FOUR          11/09/73                                                    PAGE   1
     GR 0-7  CC00 2A00  CC00 29D8  40404040  0000 0244   FFFFF14B  40404040  40404040  40404040
     GR 8-F  40404040   4C404040   40404040  4000 2832   40404040  40404C40  40404040  40404040  ⎫
     FP REG  42F00000   C0000C00   42F00000  00000000    BEBB9000  0000CCC0  00000000  00000000  ⎬ #5
                                                                                                 ⎭
     C029C0                        0000 2838                                              ....
```

```
              FOUR          11/09/73                                                    PAGE   1
     GR 0-7  CC00 29F8  CC00 29D8  40404040  0000 0244   FFFFF14B  40404C40  40404040  40404040
     GR 8-F  40404040   4C404040   40404040  4000 2832   40404040  40404040  40404040  40404040  ⎫
     FP REG  42F00000   C0000C00   42F00000  00000000    BEBB9000  0000CCC0  00000000  00000000  ⎬ #6
                                                                                                 ⎭
     C028F0                        03765D 40  00000000  0000 580C  F0F5F8C0                ... ........058.
```

              A=434E   B=376N   A+B=C58&   ⟶ ANSWER

Program Five
Addition in Binary with Minor Editing

In this program, two numbers are added (as in Program FOUR) except that some minor editing was done to express the numbers in more reasonable form for output, i.e., as numbers, not combinations of numbers and letters as in the preceding programs.

To accomplish this purpose, subroutines were used (1) to place minus signs where needed, and (2) to remove the sign nibbles C and D from the zoned numbers and replace them by F's. (A nibble is the leftmost or rightmost half of a byte.) As noted previously, a number like

F1F2F3F3

prints as 1233, whereas the number

F1F2F3D3

prints as 123L. It should be caused to print as -1233 (because of the D nibble).

PDUMPs have been included to enable the reader to trace the effect of subroutines NRTNA, NRTNB, and NRTNC. In brief, the subroutines tested the numbers by an LTR instruction to find out whether they were negative, placing a minus sign for the negatives, then removing the zone parts of the sign byte, replacing these by F's.

The flowchart is as follows:

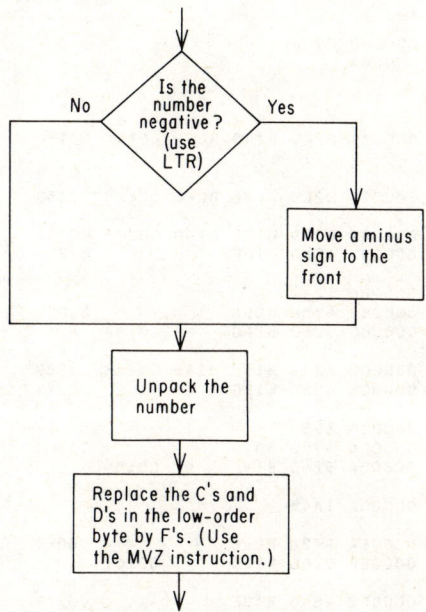

The answer, on page 32, is now readable but it is not in the best possible form. The EDMK method, to be demonstrated in the next program, is a much better method.

```
// JOB FIVE                                          12.09.46
* ADDITION IN BINARY WITH MINOR EDITING
// OPTION LINK                                                        010
// EXEC ASSEMBLY                                                      020


   LOC    OBJECT CODE      ADDR1 ADDR2   STMT    SOURCE STATEMENT                              FDOS CL3-9 11/09/73

                                           1  * THE INPUT WAS 2 CARDS - THE FIRST HAD 12345 IN CC 1-10 AND
                                           2  * THE SECOND HAD -3502 IN CC 1-10, BOTH RIGHT-ADJUSTED.
                                           3           PRINT NOGEN                                             030
   000000                                  4  FIVE     START                                                   040
                                           5  *                                    DTF SECTION                 050
                                           6  CARDF    DTFCD DEVADDR=SYSRDR,IOAREA1=CARD,EOFADDR=INEND          060
                                          27  PRINTF   DTFPR DEVADDR=SYSLST,BLKSIZE=132,IOAREA1=PRTOUT,CONTROL=YES 070
                                          48  *                                    HOUSEKEEPING SECTION        080
   000068 05B0                             49  HSKP     BALR  11,0                                             090
   00006A                                  50           USING *,11                                             100
                                          51           OPEN  CARDF,PRINTF                                      110
                                          60  *                                    PROCEDURE SECTION           120
                                          61           GET   CARDF                                             130
   00008A D209 B140 B0E6  001AA 00150      66           MVC   AOUT,X              F0F0F0F0F0F1F2F3F4F5           140
                                          67  *                                                                150
                                          68           GET   CARDF
   00009C D2C9 B14F B0E6  00189 00150      73           MVC   BOUT,X              F0F0F0F0F0F0F3F5F0D2           170
                                          74  *                                                                180
   0000A2 F279 B1BE B140  00228 001AA      75           PACK  PK,AOUT                                          190
   0000A8 4F40 B1BE       00228            76           CVB   4,PK                                             200
                                          77           PDUMP AOUT,DUMMY   }#1
   0000B6 1244                             82           LTR   4,4                                              210
   0000B8 47B0 B056             000C0      83           BNM   NRTNA                                            220
   0000BC 9260 B140       001AA            84           MVI   AOUT,C'-'                                        230
                                          85  *                                                                240
   0000C0 F279 B1BE B14F  00228 00189      86  NRTNA    PACK  PK,BOUT                                          250
   0000C6 4F50 B1BE       00228            87           CVB   5,PK                                             260
                                          88           PDUMP AOUT,DUMMY   }#2
   0000D4 1255                             93           LTR   5,5                                              270
   0000D6 47B0 B074             000DE      94           BNM   NRTNB                                            280
   0000DA 9260 B14F       00189            95           MVI   BOUT,C'-'                                        290
                                          96  *                                                                300
   0000DE 1A45                             97  NRTNB    AR    4,5                                              310
                                          98           PDUMP AOUT,DUMMY   }#3
   0000EA 47B0 B088             000F2     103           BNM   NRTNC                                            320
   0000EE 9260 B15D       001C7           104           MVI   COUT,C'-'                                        330
                                         105  *                                                                340
   0000F2 4E40 B1BE       00228           106  NRTNC    CVD   4,PK                                             350
   0000F6 F397 B15D B1BE  001C7 00228     107           UNPK  COUT,PK                                          360
                                         108           PDUMP AOUT,DUMMY   }#4
   000106 D3C0 B149 B1F6  001B3 00260     113           MVZ   AOUT+9(1),=X'F0'                                 370
   00010C D3C0 B158 B1F6  001C2 00260     114           MVZ   BOUT+9(1),=X'F0'                                 380
   000112 D3C0 B166 B1F6  001D0 00260     115           MVZ   COUT+9(1),=X'F0'                                 390
                                         116           PDUMP AOUT,DUMMY   }#5                                  390
                                         121           CNTRL PRINTF,SK,1                                       390
                                         127           PUT   PRINTF                                            400
                                         132  INEND    CLOSE CARDF,PRINTF                                      410
                                         141           EOJ                                                     420
                                         144  *                                    AREA                        430
   000150                                145  CARD     DS    0CL80                                             440
   000150                                146  X        DS    ZL10                                              450
```

30

```
LOC      OBJECT CODE        ADDR1 ADDR2  STMT       SOURCE STATEMENT                              FDOS CL3-9 11/09/73

00015A                                    147              DS      CL70                            460
0001A0                                    148 PRTOUT       DS      0CL132                          470
0001A0   E3C8C540E2E4D440                 149              DC      CL10'THE SUM OF'                480
0001AA                                    150 AOUT         DS      ZL10                            490
0001B4   40C1D5C440                       151              DC      CL5' AND '                      500
0001B9                                    152 BOUT         DS      ZL10                            510
0001C3   40C9E240                         153              DC      CL4' IS '                       520
0001C7                                    154 COUT         DS      ZL10                            530
0001D1   4040404040404040                 155              DC      CL83' '                         540
000228                                    156 PK           DS      D                               550
000230                                    157 DUMMY        DS      CL1                             555
000068                                    158              END     HSKP                            560
000238   5B5BC2D6D7C5D540                 159                      =C'$$BOPEN '
000240   5B5BC2D7C4E4D4D7                 160                      =CL8'$$BPDUMP'
000248   000001AA00000230                 161                      =A(AOUT,DUMMY)
000250   5B5BC2C3D3D6E2C5                 162                      =C'$$BCLOSE'
000258   00000000                         163                      =A(CARDF)
00025C   00000038                         164                      =A(PRINTF)
000260   F0                               165                      =X'F0'


         FIVE                 11/09/73                                                               PAGE    1

GR 0-7   00002A48 C0002A40 0000FFFF 00002800   00003039 FFFFFF7C 00000000 000027B8
GR 8-F   0C00430A 0A0107F1 00002810 4000286A   000037D8 000047D8 A000289C 0C002A68         }#1
FP REG   42F00000 C0000000 42F00000 00000000   BEBB9000 000000C0 00000000 00000000

0029A0                     D6C64040 404040F1   F2F3F4F5 40C1D5C4 40404040 404040F3            OF      1    2345 AND       3
0029C0   F5F0D240 C9E24040 40404040 40404040   5B404040 40404040 40404040 40404040      50K IS       $
0029E0   40404040 --SAME--
002A20   40404040 47F0F01A 00000000 0012345F                                                  .00.........


         FIVE                 11/09/73                                                               PAGE    1

GR 0-7   00002A48 C0002A40 0000FFFF 00002800   00003039 FFFFF252 00000000 000027B8
GR 8-F   0C00430A 0A0107F1 0C002810 4000286A   000037D8 0C0047D8 A000289C 0C002A68         }#2
FP REG   42F00000 C0000000 42F00000 00000000   BEBB9000 000000C0 00000000 00000000

0029A0                     D6C64040 404040F1   F2F3F4F5 40C1D5C4 40404040 404040F3            OF      1    2345 AND       3
0029C0   F5F0D240 C9E24040 40404040 40404040   5B404040 40404040 40404040 40404040      50K IS       $
0029E0   40404040 --SAME--
002A20   40404040 47F0F01A 00000000 0003502D                                                  .00........&.
```

```
          FIVE          11/09/73                                                                    PAGE    1

   GR 0-7  CC002A48 C0002A40 0000FFFF 00002800   0000228B FFFFF252 00000000 000027B8                         ⎫
   GR 8-F  0C00430A 0A0107F1 00002810 4000286A   000037D8 000047D8 A000289C 00002A68                         ⎬ #3
   FP REG  42F00000 C000CC00 42F00000 00000000   BEBB9000 00000000 00000000 00000000                         ⎭

   0029A0                    D6C64040 404040F1   F2F3F4F5 40C1D5C4 40604040 404040F3        OF    1 2345 AND -    3
   0029C0  F5F0D240 C9E24040 40404040 40404040   5B404040 40404040 40404040 40404040     50K IS           $
   0029E0  4C404040 --SAME--
   002A20  40404040 47F0F01A 00000000 0003502D                                               .00.......&.


          FIVE          11/09/73                                                                    PAGE    1

   GR 0-7  CC002A48 C0002A40 0000FFFF 00002800   0000228B FFFFF252 00000000 000027B8                         ⎫
   GR 8-F  0C00430A 0A0107F1 00002810 4000286A   000037D8 000047D8 A000289C 00002A68                         ⎬ #4
   FP REG  42F00000 C000C000 42F00000 00C00000   BEBB9000 00000000 00000000 00000000                         ⎭

   0029A0                    D6C64040 404040F1   F2F3F4F5 40C1D5C4 40604040 404040F3        OF    1 2345 AND -    3
   0029C0  F5F0D240 C9E240F0 F0F0F0F0 F0F8F8F4   C3404040 40404040 40404040 40404040     50K IS 000000884 C
   0029E0  40404040 --SAME--
   002A20  4C404040 47F0F01A 00000000 0008843C                                               .00.........


          FIVE          11/09/73                                                                    PAGE    1

   GR 0-7  CC002A48 C0002A40 0000FFFF 00002800   0000228B FFFFF252 00000000 000027B8                         ⎫
   GR 8-F  0C00430A 0A0107F1 00002810 4000286A   000037D8 000047D8 A000289C 00002A68                         ⎬ #5
   FP REG  42F00000 00000000 42F00000 00000000   BEBB9000 00000000 00000000 00000000                         ⎭

   0029A0                    D6C64040 404040F1   F2F3F4F5 40C1D5C4 40604040 404040F3        OF    1 2345 AND -    3
   0029C0  F5F0F240 C9E240F0 F0F0F0F0 F0F8F8F4   F3404040 40404040 40404040 40404040     502 IS 000000884 3
   0029E0  40404040 --SAME--
   002A20  40404040 47F0F01A 00000000 0008843C                                               .00.........



   THE SUM OF     12345 AND -    3502 IS 0000008843     ⎬ → ANSWER
```

Program Six

Binary Addition with EDMK

In this program, three numbers (A,B,C) are read from a card, packed, converted to binary, and the result, A + B - C, is computed. The sum is then converted from binary to packed form and edited. The EDMK instruction, explained in the Appendix, is used to obtain the answer in a satisfactory form, as seen at the bottom of page 40. Unlike the previous program, only one subroutine, RT, was needed to do all the editing. This is much easier and produces a good-looking result. The "trick" is to make a pattern large enough to fit all the numbers involved.

Twelve PDUMPs have been provided to enable the reader to follow the program step-by-step. This takes time but is worth the trouble.

The other new feature of this program is the production of a heading, using the ORG command, in statement 222. The instruction

ORG PRTOUT

requires the computer to set the location counter back to the location of PRTOUT. In statement 212, the location of PRTOUT was 000234. Notice that in statements 222 and 223, the location has been reset to 000234. The result is that the area definitions overlap, as follows:

LOC	CONTENTS
234	address of PRTOUT
23C	spaces for AOUT
244	the letter 'A'
25D	spaces for BOUT
265	the letter 'B'
27E	spaces for COUT
286	the letter 'C'
29F	spaces for ZSUM
2A7	the word 'SUM'

First the heading is printed (statement 67). This has the letters A, B, C and the word SUM. Then, these are removed from core by replacing them with blanks using an MVC. (A faster method is shown later.) Then the numbers are moved into the same area, and the results are printed. Many examples of this technique will be shown in later programs. In this program, the PDUMPs fell between the heading and the results. In normal practice, after the program is checked out, the PDUMP cards are removed and the results appear neatly edited under the proper headings.

```
// JOB SIX                                                    17.11.52
* BINARY ADDITION WITH EDMARK
// OPTION LINK                                                        020
// EXEC ASSEMBLY                                                      030


    LOC  OBJECT CODE      ADDR1 ADDR2  STMT  SOURCE STATEMENT                          FDOS CL3-9 11/12/73

                                          1 * THE INPUT IS SHOWN ON CARDS 690,700 AND 710 UNDER   AREAS
                                          2 *                                                              040
                                          3        PRINT NOGEN                                             050
    000000                                 4 SIX   START                                                   060
                                          5 *                                      DTF SECTION             070
                                          6 CARDF DTFCD DEVADDR=SYSRDR,IOAREA1=CARDIN,EOFADDR=INEND        080
                                         27 PRINTF DTFPR BLKSIZE=132,DEVADDR=SYSLST,IOAREA1=PRTOUT,CONTROL=YES 110
                                         48 *                                      HOUSEKEEPING SECTION    130
    000068 05B0                          49 BEGIN BALR  11,0                                               140
    00006A                               50        USING *,11                                              150
                                         51        OPEN  CARDF,PRINTF                                      160
                                         60 *                                      HEADING                 170
                                         61        CNTRL PRINTF,SK,1               SKIP TO TOP OF PAGE     180
                                         67       (PUT   PRINTF)                   HEADING - A,B,C,SUM     190
                                         72        CNTRL PRINTF,SP,2               SPACE 2 (EXTRA) LINES   200
    0000A6 D283 B1CA B24E 00234 00288    78        MVC   PRTOUT,BLANKS             CLEANS OUTPUT AREA      210
                                         79 * A MUCH BETTER WAY TO ACCOMPLISH THE SAME PURPOSE IS TO USE THE
                                         80 * INSTRUCTION    XC PRTOUT,PRTOUT WHICH WE WILL TAKE UP LATER
                                         81 *                                      PROCEDURE SECTION       220
                                         82        GET   CARDF                     READS A,B AND C         230
                                         87        PDUMP A,PAT  ←#1
                                         92 *                                                              240
    0000C2 F259 B2D2 B17A 0033C 001E4    93        PACK  PKA,A                                              250
    0000C8 D205 B2EA B2D2 00354 0033C    94        MVC   PK,PKA                                             260
                                         95        PDUMP A,PAT  ←#2
    0000D8 45A0 B15E           001C8    100        BAL   10,RT                     EDITS A                  270
    0000DC D20E B1D2 B307 0023C 00371   101        MVC   AOUT,WORK                                          280
                                        102        PDUMP A,PAT  ←#3
                                        107 *                                                              290
    0000EC F259 B2DA B184 00344 001EE   108        PACK  PKB,B                                              300
    0000F2 D205 B2EA B2DA 00354 00344   109        MVC   PK,PKB                                             310
                                        110        PDUMP A,PAT  ←#4
    000102 45A0 B15E           001C8    115        BAL   10,RT                     EDITS B                  320
    000106 D20E B1F3 B307 0025D 00371   116        MVC   BOUT,WORK                                          330
                                        117        PDUMP A,PAT  ←#5
                                        122 *                                                              340
    000116 F259 B2E2 B18E 0034C 001F8   123        PACK  PKC,C                                              350
    00011C D205 B2EA B2E2 00354 0034C   124        MVC   PK,PKC                                             360
                                        125        PDUMP A,PAT  ←#6
    00012C 45A0 B15E           001C8    130        BAL   10,RT                     EDITS C                  370
    000130 D20E B214 B307 0027E 00371   131        MVC   COUT,WORK                                          380
                                        132        PDUMP A,PAT  ←#7
                                        137 *                                                              390
    000140 F875 B2FE B2D2 00368 0033C   138        ZAP   DOUBLE,PKA                                         400
    000146 4F40 B2FE           00368    139        CVB   4,DOUBLE                  A IN GPR 4               410
                                        140        PDUMP A,PAT  ←#8
    000154 F875 B2FE B2DA 00368 00344   145        ZAP   DOUBLE,PKB                                         420
    00015A 4F50 B2FE           00368    146        CVB   5,DOUBLE                  B IN GPR 5               430
                                        147        PDUMP A,PAT  ←#9
                                        152 *                                                              440
    000168 1A45                         153        AR    4,5                       A+B IN GPR 4             450
```

```
LOC     OBJECT CODE      ADDR1 ADDR2   STMT    SOURCE STATEMENT                                        FDOS CL3-9  11/12/73

                                        154 *
00016A  F875 B2FE B2E2   00368 0034C    155           ZAP     DOUBLE,PKC                                              460
000170  4F50 B2FE              00368    156           CVB     5,DOUBLE            C IN GPR 5                          470
                                        157           PDUMP   A,PAT  ←—#10                                            480
                                        162 *                                                                         490
00017E  1B45                             163           SR      4,5                 A+B-C IN GPR 4                      500
                                        164 *                                                                         510
000180  4E40 B2F6              00360    165           CVD     4,SUM                                                   520
000184  F857 B2EA B2F6   00354 00360    166           ZAP     PK,SUM              SUM IN PACKED FORM                  530
                                        167           PDUMP   A,PAT  ←—#11
000194  45A0 B15E              001C8    172           BAL     10,RT               EDITS SUM                           540
000198  D20E B235 B307   0029F 00371    173           MVC     ZSUM,WORK                                               550
                                        174           PDUMP   A,PAT  ←—#12
                                        179 *                                                                         560
                                        180           PUT     PRINTF                                                  570
                                        185 INEND     CLOSE   CARDF,PRINTF                                            580
                                        194           EOJ                                                             590
                                        197 *                                     SUBROUTINE                          600
0001C8  D20E B307 B316   00371 00380    198 RT        MVC     WORK,PAT                                                610
0001CE  4110 B313              0037D    199           LA      1,WORK+12           ADDRESS OF DECIMAL POINT            620
0001D2  DF0E B307 B2EA   00371 00354    200           EDMK    WORK,PK                                                 630
0001D8  4780 B178              001E2    201           BNM     POS                                                     640
0001DC  0610                             202           BCTR    1,0                                                    650
                                        203 * AN ALTERNATE WOULD BE    SH  1,=H'1'
0001DE  9260 1000              00000    204           MVI     0(1),C'-'           PLACES MINUS SIGN IF NECESSARY      660
0001E2  07FA                             205 POS       BR      10                                                      670
                                        206 *                                     AREA                                680
0001E4                                   207 CARDIN    DS      0CL80                                                   690
0001E4                                   208 A         DS      ZL10                -92,345.67                          690
0001EE                                   209 B         DS      ZL10                -91,238.42                          700
0001F8                                   210 C         DS      ZL10                 23,764.92                          710
000202                                   211           DS      CL50                                                    730
000234                                   212 PRTOUT    DS      0CL132                                                  740
000234  4040404040404040                 213           DC      16C' '                                                  750
000244  C1                                214           DC      C'A'                                                   760
000245  4040404040404040                 215           DC      32C' '                                                  770
000265  C2                                216           DC      C'B'                                                   780
000266  4040404040404040                 217           DC      32C' '                                                  790
000286  C3                                218           DC      C'C'                                                   800
000287  4040404040404040                 219           DC      32C' '                                                  810
0002A7  E2E4D4                            220           DC      CL3'SUM'                                               820
0002AA  4040404040404040                 221           DC      14C' '                                                  830
000234                                   222           ORG     PRTOUT                                                  831
000234                                   223           DS      CL8                                                     832
00023C                                   224 AOUT      DS      CL15                                                    833
00024B                                   225           DS      CL18                                                    834
00025D                                   226 BOUT      DS      CL15                                                    835
00026C                                   227           DS      CL18                                                    836
00027E                                   228 COUT      DS      CL15                                                    837
00028D                                   229           DS      CL18                                                    838
00029F                                   230 ZSUM      DS      CL15                                                    839
```

```
   LOC    OBJECT CODE      ADDR1 ADDR2  STMT   SOURCE STATEMENT                                FDOS CL3-9 11/12/73

  0002AE                                 231          DS    CL10                                840
  0002B8  4040404040404040                232 BLANKS  DC    132C' '                             840
  00033C                                  233         DS    0F
  00033C                                  234 PKA     DS    PL6                                 850
  000344                                  235         DS    0F
  000344                                  236 PKB     DS    PL6                                 860
  00034C                                  237         DS    0F
  00034C                                  238 PKC     DS    PL6                                 870
  000354                                  239         DS    0F
  000354                                  240 PK      DS    PL6                                 880
  000360                                  241 SUM     DS    D                                   890
  000368                                  242 DOUBLE  DS    D                                   895
  000370                                  243 DUMMY   DS    CL1                                 896
  000371                                  244 WORK    DS    CL15                                900
  000380  402020206B202020                245 PAT     DC    X'402020206B2020206B2020214B2020'   910
                                          246 *               B C D D , D D D , D D ( . D D    915
  000068                                  247         END   BEGIN                               930
  000390  5B5BC2D6D7C5D540                248         =C'$$BOPEN '
  000398  5B5BC2D7C4E4D4D7                249         =CL8'$$BPDUMP'
  0003A0  CCC001E400000380                250         =A(A,PAT)
  0003A8  5B5BC2C3D3D6E2C5                251         =C'$$BCLOSE'
  0003B0  00C00038                        252         =A(PRINTF)
  0003B4  00C00000                        253         =A(CARDF)
```

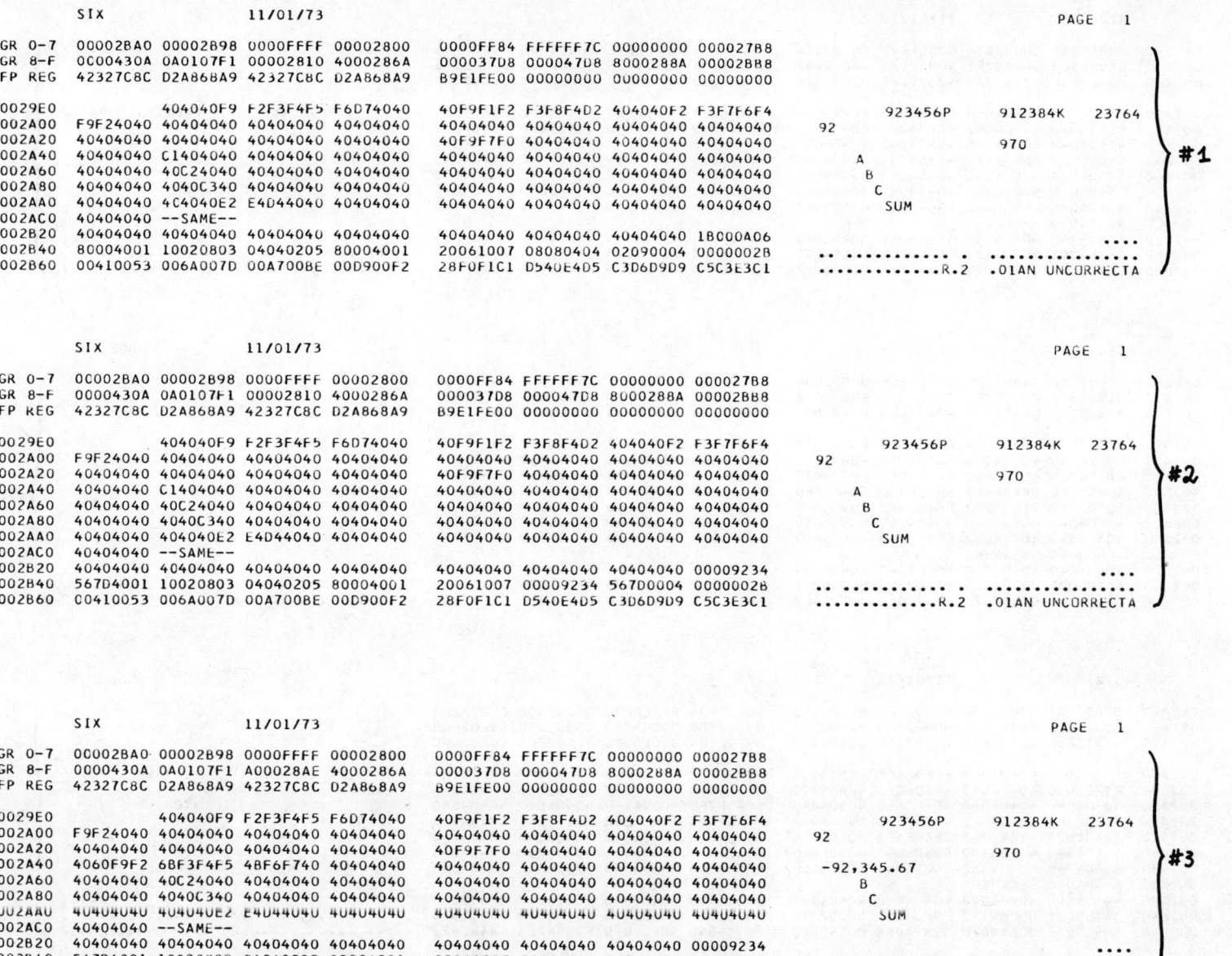

```
          SIX            11/01/73                                                                    PAGE   1

 GR 0-7   00002BA0 00002B98 0000FFFF 00002800   0000FF84 FFFFFF7C 00000000 000027B8
 GR 8-F   0000430A 0A0107F1 A00028AE 4000286A   000037D8 000047D8 8000288A 00002BB8
 FP REG   42327C8C D2A868A9 42327C8C D2A868A9   B9E1FE00 00000000 00000000 00000000

 0029E0            404040F9 F2F3F4F5 F6D74040   40F9F1F2 F3F8F4D2 404040F2 F3F7F6F4           923456P     912384K    23764
 002A00   F9F24040 40404040 40404040 40404040   40404040 40404040 40404040 40404040    92
 002A20   40404040 40404040 40404040 40404040   40F9F7F0 40404040 40404040 40404040                      970
 002A40   4060F9F2 6BF3F4F5 4BF6F740 40404040   40404040 40404040 40404040 40404040          -92,345.67                       }  #4
 002A60   40404040 40C24040 40404040 40404040   40404040 40404040 40404040 40404040             B
 002A80   40404040 4040C340 40404040 40404040   40404040 40404040 40404040 40404040             C
 002AA0   40404040 4C4040E2 E4D44040 40404040   40404040 40404040 40404040 40404040            SUM
 002AC0   40404040 --SAME--
 002B20   40404040 40404040 40404040 40404040   40404040 40404040 40404040 00009234                                    ....
 002B40   567D4001 00009123 842D0205 80004001   20061007 00009123 842D0004 0000002B    ...............       ...............
 002B60   00410053 006A007D 00A700BE 00D900F2   28404040 404060F9 F26BF3F4 F54BF6F7    ............R.2  .        -92,345.67


          SIX            11/01/73                                                                    PAGE   1

 GR 0-7   00002BA0 00002B98 0000FFFF 00002800   0000FF84 FFFFFF7C 00000000 000027B8
 GR 8-F   0000430A 0A0107F1 900028D8 4000286A   000037D8 000047D8 8000288A 00002BB8
 FP REG   42327C8C D2A868A9 42327C8C D2A868A9   B9E1FE00 00000000 00000000 00000000

 0029E0            404040F9 F2F3F4F5 F6D74040   40F9F1F2 F3F8F4D2 404040F2 F3F7F6F4           923456P     912384K    23764
 002A00   F9F24040 40404040 40404040 40404040   40404040 40404040 40404040 40404040    92
 002A20   40404040 40404040 40404040 40404040   40F9F7F0 40404040 40404040 40404040                      970
 002A40   4060F9F2 6BF3F4F5 4BF6F740 40404040   40404040 40404040 40404040 40404040          -92,345.67
 002A60   404060F9 F16BF2F3 F84BF4F2 40404040   40404040 40404040 40404040 40404040          -91,238.42                       }  #5
 002A80   40404040 4040C340 40404040 40404040   40404040 40404040 40404040 40404040             C
 002AA0   40404040 4C4040E2 E4D44040 40404040   40404040 40404040 40404040 40404040            SUM
 002AC0   40404040 --SAME--
 002B20   40404040 40404040 40404040 40404040   40404040 40404040 40404040 00009234                                    ....
 002B40   567D4001 00009123 842D0205 80004001   20061007 00009123 842D0004 0000002B    ...............       ...............
 002B60   00410053 006A007D 00A700BE 00D900F2   28404040 404060F9 F16BF2F3 F84BF4F2    ............R.2  .        -91,238.42


          SIX            11/01/73                                                                    PAGE   1

 GR 0-7   00002BA0 00002B98 0000FFFF 00002800   0000FF84 FFFFFF7C 00000000 000027B8
 GR 8-F   0000430A 0A0107F1 900028D8 4000286A   000037D8 000047D8 8000288A 00002BB8
 FP REG   42327C8C D2A868A9 42327C8C D2A868A9   B9E1FE00 00000000 00000000 00000000

 0029E0            404040F9 F2F3F4F5 F6D74040   40F9F1F2 F3F8F4D2 404040F2 F3F7F6F4           923456P     912384K    23764
 002A00   F9F24040 40404040 40404040 40404040   40404040 40404040 40404040 40404040    92
 002A20   40404040 40404040 40404040 40404040   40F9F7F0 40404040 40404040 40404040                      970
 002A40   4060F9F2 6BF3F4F5 4BF6F740 40404040   40404040 40404040 40404040 40404040          -92,345.67
 002A60   404060F9 F16BF2F3 F84BF4F2 40404040   40404040 40404040 40404040 40404040          -91,238.42                       }  #6
 002A80   40404040 4040C340 40404040 40404040   40404040 40404040 40404040 40404040             C
 002AA0   40404040 404040E2 E4D44040 40404040   40404040 40404040 40404040 40404040            SUM
 002AC0   40404040 --SAME--
 002B20   40404040 40404040 40404040 40404040   40404040 40404040 40404040 00009234                                    ....
 002B40   567D4001 00009123 842D0205 00002376   492F1007 00002376 492F0004 0000002B    ...............       ...............
 002B60   00410053 006A007D 00A700BE 00D900F2   28404040 404060F9 F16BF2F3 F84BF4F2    ............R.2  .        -91,238.42
```

```
              SIX           11/01/73                                                                                    PAGE     1

    GR  0-7   00002BA0 00002B98 0000FFFF 00002800   0000FF84 FFFFFF7C 00000000 000027B8                              ⎫
    GR  8-F   0000430A 0A0107F1 90002902 4000286A   000037D8 000047D8 8000288A 00002BB8                              ⎪
    FP REG    42327C8C D2A868A9 42327C8C D2A868A9   B9E1FE00 00000000 00000000 00000000                              ⎪
                                                                                                                     ⎪
    0029E0             404040F9 F2F3F4F5 F6D74040   40F9F1F2 F3F8F4D2 404040F2 F3F7F6F4           923456P   912384K     23764  ⎪
    002A00    F9F24040 40404040 40404040 40404040   40404040 40404040 40404040 40404040        92                              ⎪
    002A20    40404040 40404040 40404040 40404040   40F9F7F0 40404040 40404040 40404040                     970                ⎬ #7
    002A40    4060F9F2 6BF3F4F5 4BF6F740 40404040   40404040 40404040 40404040 40404040        -92,345.67                      ⎪
    002A60    404060F9 F16BF2F3 F84BF4F2 40404040   40404040 40404040 40404040 40404040        -91,238.42                      ⎪
    002A80    40404040 F2F36BF7 F6F44BF9 F2404040   40404040 40404040 40404040 40404040         23,764.92                      ⎪
    002AA0    40404040 4C4040E2 E4D44040 40404040   40404040 40404040 40404040 40404040           SUM                          ⎪
    002AC0    40404040 --SAME--                                                                                                ⎪
    002B20    40404040 40404040 40404040 40404040   40404040 40404040 40404040 00009234                              ....      ⎪
    002B40    567D4001 00009123 842D0205 00002376   492F1007 00002376 492F0004 0000002B        .. ............... ...............⎪
    002B60    00410053 006A007D 00A700BE 00D900F2   28404040 404040F2 F36BF7F6 F44BF9F2        ................R.2 .    23,764.92 ⎭


              SIX           11/01/73                                                                                    PAGE     1

    GR  0-7   00002BA0 00002B98 0000FFFF 00002800   FF731779 FFFFFF7C 00000000 000027B8                              ⎫
    GR  8-F   0000430A 0A0107F1 90002902 4000286A   000037D8 000047D8 8000288A 00002BB8                              ⎪
    FP REG    42327C8C D2A868A9 42327C8C D2A868A9   B9E1FE00 00000000 00000000 00000000                              ⎪
                                                                                                                     ⎪
    0029E0             404040F9 F2F3F4F5 F6D74040   40F9F1F2 F3F8F4D2 404040F2 F3F7F6F4           923456P   912384K     23764  ⎪
    002A00    F9F24040 40404040 40404040 40404040   40404040 40404040 40404040 40404040        92                              ⎪
    002A20    40404040 40404040 40404040 40404040   40F9F7F0 40404040 40404040 40404040                     970                ⎬ #8
    002A40    4060F9F2 6BF3F4F5 4BF6F740 40404040   40404040 40404040 40404040 40404040        -92,345.67                      ⎪
    002A60    404060F9 F16BF2F3 F84BF4F2 40404040   40404040 40404040 40404040 40404040        -91,238.42                      ⎪
    002A80    40404040 F2F36BF7 F6F44BF9 F2404040   40404040 40404040 40404040 40404040         23,764.92                      ⎪
    002AA0    40404040 404040E2 E4D44040 40404040   40404040 40404040 40404040 40404040           SUM                          ⎪
    002AC0    40404040 --SAME--                                                                                                ⎪
    002B20    40404040 40404040 40404040 40404040   40404040 40404040 40404040 00009234                              ....      ⎪
    002B40    567D4001 00009123 842D0205 00002376   492F1007 00002376 492F0004 0000002B        .. ............... ...............⎪
    002B60    00410053 006A007D 00000000 9234567D   28404040 404040F2 F36BF7F6 F44BF9F2        ................  .       23,764.92 ⎭


              SIX           11/01/73                                                                                    PAGE     1

    GR  0-7   00002BA0 00002B98 0000FFFF 00002800   FF731779 FF74C7FE 00000000 000027B8                              ⎫
    GR  8-F   0000430A 0A0107F1 90002902 4000286A   000037D8 000047D8 8000288A 00002BB8                              ⎪
    FP REG    42327C8C D2A868A9 42327C8C D2A868A9   B9E1FE00 00000000 00000000 00000000                              ⎪
                                                                                                                     ⎪
    0029E0             404040F9 F2F3F4F5 F6D74040   40F9F1F2 F3F8F4D2 404040F2 F3F7F6F4           923456P   912384K     23764  ⎪
    002A00    F9F24040 40404040 40404040 40404040   40404040 40404040 40404040 40404040        92                              ⎪
    002A20    40404040 40404040 40404040 40404040   40F9F7F0 40404040 40404040 40404040                     970                ⎬ #9
    002A40    4060F9F2 6BF3F4F5 4BF6F740 40404040   40404040 40404040 40404040 40404040        -92,345.67                      ⎪
    002A60    404060F9 F16BF2F3 F84BF4F2 40404040   40404040 40404040 40404040 40404040        -91,238.42                      ⎪
    002A80    40404040 F2F36BF7 F6F44BF9 F2404040   40404040 40404040 40404040 40404040         23,764.92                      ⎪
    002AA0    40404040 404040E2 E4D44040 40404040   40404040 40404040 40404040 40404040           SUM                          ⎪
    002AC0    40404040 --SAME--                                                                                                ⎪
    002B20    40404040 40404040 40404040 40404040   40404040 40404040 40404040 00009234                              ....      ⎪
    002B40    567D4001 00009123 842D0205 00002376   492F1007 00002376 492F0004 0000002B        .. ............... ...............⎪
    002B60    00410053 006A007D 00000000 9123842D   28404040 404040F2 F36BF7F6 F44BF9F2        ................  .       23,764.92 ⎭
```

```
         SIX              11/01/73                                                              PAGE   1

         GR 0-7   0C002BA0 00002B98 0000FFFF 00002800   FEE7DF77 0024432C 00000000 000027B8
         GR 8-F   0000430A 0A0107F1 90002902 4000286A   000037D8 000047D8 8000288A 00002BB8
         FP REG   42327C8C D2A868A9 42327C8C D2A868A9   B9E1FE00 00000000 00000000 00000000

         0029E0            404040F9 F2F3F4F5 F6D74040   40F9F1F2 F3F8F4D2 404040F2 F3F7F6F4              923456P       912384K      23764
         002A00   F9F24040 40404040 40404040 40404040   40404040 40404040 40404040 40404040      92
         002A20   40404040 40404040 40404040 40404040   40F9F7F0 40404040 40404040 40404040                            970
         002A40   4060F9F2 6BF3F4F5 4BF6F740 40404040   40404040 40404040 40404040 40404040     -92,345.67                                        }
         002A60   404060F9 F16BF2F3 F34BF4F2 40404040   40404040 40404040 40404040 40404040     -91,238.42                                        } #10
         002A80   40404040 F2F36BF7 F6F44BF9 F2404040   40404040 40404040 40404040 40404040      23,764.92                                        }
         002AA0   40404040 404040E2 E4D44040 40404040   40404040 40404040 40404040 40404040         SUM
         002AC0   40404040 --SAME--
         002B20   40404040 40404040 40404040 40404040   40404040 40404040 40404040 00009234                                              ....
         002B40   567D4001 00009123 842D0205 00002376   492F1007 00002376 492F0004 0000002B     .. ............. . ...............
         002B60   00410053 006A007D 00000000 2376492C   28404040 404040F2 F36BF7F6 F44BF9F2     ................ .               23,764.92

         SIX              11/01/73                                                              PAGE   1

         GR 0-7   00002BA0 00002B98 0000FFFF 00002800   FEC39C4B 0024432C 00000000 000027B8
         GR 8-F   0000430A 0A0107F1 90002902 4000286A   000037D8 000047D8 8000288A 00002BB8
         FP REG   42327C8C D2A868A9 42327C8C D2A868A9   B9E1FE00 00000000 00000000 00000000

         0029E0            404040F9 F2F3F4F5 F6D74040   40F9F1F2 F3F8F4D2 404040F2 F3F7F6F4              923456P       912384K      23764
         002A00   F9F24040 40404040 40404040 40404040   40404040 40404040 40404040 40404040      92
         002A20   40404040 40404040 40404040 40404040   40F9F7F0 40404040 40404040 40404040                            970
         002A40   4060F9F2 6BF3F4F5 4BF6F740 40404040   40404040 40404040 40404040 40404040     -92,345.67                                        }
         002A60   404060F9 F16BF2F3 F84BF4F2 40404040   40404040 40404040 40404040 40404040     -91,238.42                                        } #11
         002A80   40404040 F2F36BF7 F6F44BF9 F2404040   40404040 40404040 40404040 40404040      23,764.92                                        }
         002AA0   40404040 404040E2 E4D44040 40404040   40404040 40404040 40404040 40404040         SUM
         002AC0   40404040 --SAME--
         002B20   40404040 40404040 40404040 40404040   40404040 40404040 40404040 00009234                                              ....
         002B40   567D4001 00009123 842D0205 00002376   492F1007 00020734 901D0004 0000002B     .. ............. . ...............
         002B60   00000002 0734901D 00000000 2376492C   28404040 404040F2 F36BF7F6 F44BF9F2     ................ .               23,764.92

         SIX              11/01/73                                                              PAGE   1

         GR 0-7   00002BA0 00002B98 0000FFFF 00002800   FEC39C4B 0024432C 00000000 000027B8
         GR 8-F   0000430A 0A0107F1 9000296A 4000286A   000037D8 000047D8 8000288A 00002BB8
         FP REG   42327C8C D2A868A9 42327C8C D2A868A9   B9E1FE00 00000000 00000000 00000000

         0029E0            404040F9 F2F3F4F5 F6D74040   40F9F1F2 F3F8F4D2 404040F2 F3F7F6F4              923456P       912384K      23764
         002A00   F9F24040 40404040 40404040 40404040   40404040 40404040 40404040 40404040      92
         002A20   40404040 40404040 40404040 40404040   40F9F7F0 40404040 40404040 40404040                            970
         002A40   4060F9F2 6BF3F4F5 4BF6F740 40404040   40404040 40404040 40404040 40404040     -92,345.67
         002A60   404060F9 F16BF2F3 F84BF4F2 40404040   40404040 40404040 40404040 40404040     -91,238.42                                        } #12
         002A80   40404040 F2F36BF7 F6F44BF9 F2404040   40404040 40404040 40404040 40404040      23,764.92
         002AA0   40404060 F2F0F76B F3F4F94B F0F14040   40404040 40404040 40404040 40404040    -207,349.01
         002AC0   40404040 --SAME--
         002B20   40404040 40404040 40404040 40404040   40404040 40404040 40404040 00009234                                              ....
         002B40   567D4001 00009123 842D0205 00002376   492F1007 00020734 901D0004 0000002B     .. ............. . ...............
         002B60   00000002 0734901D 00000000 2376492C   28404040 4060F2F0 F76BF3F4 F94BF0F1     ................ .              -207,349.01
```

        A   B   C   SUM ← *The heading (moved)*

   -92,345.67   -91,238.42   23,764.92   -207,349.01 ← *Answers*

Program Seven
Binary Multiplication

In this program, the problem is to multiply two numbers and print the numbers and the product under a heading. The first number is of the form: (3).(2), which means that there are three digits before the decimal point and two digits after the decimal point. The second number is of the form (4).(1). The product, therefore, can be no bigger than (3 + 4).(2 + 1), or (7).(3).

To edit the product (the largest of the numbers), its size in packed form must be calculated. This is not too difficult. It will be of the form

0x xx xx xx͜xx xS

where the symbol ͜ means "implied decimal point" and the symbol "S" means the sign nibble which in this case will be a D because the answer is negative. (It would be a C if the answer were positive.) The 0 is there to fill out the high-order byte. Note that there are 7 x's before the (implied) decimal point and 3 x's after it. This calculation determines the size of PK (see statement 164) and of the pattern (see statement 165). In statement 165, note that there are 7 D's before the decimal point and 3 D's after it.

In order to make the original numbers fit the pattern, some pre-editing must be done. Otherwise, a different pattern would have to be used for each number. Consider the first number which happens to be -813.76. This is of the form (3).(2), and must be changed to (7).(3). The steps are as follows:

STMT 84. The number is packed: 81 37 6C

STMT 85. PK becomes 00 00 00 00 00 00

STMT 86. The three-byte number is moved into the third, fourth, and fifth bytes of PK:

00 00 81 3͜7 6C 00

STMT 87. The sign nibble is moved:

00 00 81 3͜7 6C̄ 0C

STMT 88. The number is moved with offset in order to get three digits after the implied decimal point. The result is

00 00 08 13͜76 CC

STMT 89. Now the first of the two C's is replaced by a 0. For an explanation of the NI instruction see the Appendix. The result is

00 00 08 13͜76 0C

which is in the proper form for editing with the pattern.

This is not fun, but it is necessary to produce the pretty result on page 44.

```
// JOB SEVEN                                          17.51.12
*  BINARY MULTIPLICATION
// OPTION LINK                                                  020
// EXEC ASSEMBLY                                                030
```

PAGE   1

```
   LOC    OBJECT CODE    ADDR1  ADDR2  STMT   SOURCE STATEMENT                              FDOS CL3-9 11/01/73
                                         1           PRINT  NOGEN                                              040
   000000                                2    SEVEN  START                                                     050
                                         3    *                             DTF SECTION                        060
                                         4    CARD   DTFCD  DEVADDR=SYSRDR,IOAREA1=IN,EOFADDR=ENDUP            080
                                        25    LISTER DTFPR  BLKSIZE=132,DEVADDR=SYSLST,IOAREA1=OUTPUT,CONTROL=YES  100
                                        46    *                             HOUSEKEEPING SECTION               120
   000068 05B0                          47    ANFANG BALR   11,0                                               130
   00006A                               48           USING  *,11                                               140
                                        49           OPEN   CARD,LISTER                                        150
                                        58    *                             PROCEDURE SECTION                  160
                                        59           CNTRL  LISTER,SK,1            SKIP TO TOP OF PAGE         170
                                        65           PUT    LISTER                 HEADING                     180
                                        70           CNTRL  LISTER,SP,2            SPACE TWO EXTRA LINES       190
   0000A6 D783 B156 B156 001C0 001C0    76           XC     OUTPUT,OUTPUT  ← a fast way                        200
                                        77    *                              to clear an area.                 210
                                        78           GET    CARD                   READS A AND B               220
                                        83    * THE FOLLOWING PACKS A AND PRE-EDITS TO FIT THE 15-CHARACTER PATTERN  230
   0000B8 F229 B1DA B106 00244 00170    84           PACK   PKA,A                  81 37 6S                    240
   0000BE D205 B1E0 B204 0024A 0026E    85           MVC    PK,ZEROS               CLEARS PK                   250
   0000C4 D202 B1E2 B1DA 0024C 00244    86           MVC    PK+2(3),PKA            00 00 81 37 6S 00           260
   0000CA D100 B1E5 B1E4 0024F 0024E    87           MVN    PK+5(1),PK+4           00 00 81 37 6S 0S           270
   0000D0 F132 B1E2 B1E2 0024C 0024C    88           MVO    PK+2(4),PK+2(3)        00 00 08 13 76 SS           280
   0000D6 940F B1E5      0024F          89           NI     PK+5,X'0F'             00 00 08 13 76 0S           290
   0000DA 45A0 B0EA      00154          90           BAL    10,EDRT                EDITS PKA (EXTENDED)        300
   0000DE D20D B161 B1F5 001CB 0025F    91           MVC    AOUT,WORK              A IN OUTPUT AREA            310
                                        92    * THE FOLLOWING PACKS B AND PRE-EDITS IT                         320
   0000E4 F229 B1DD B110 00247 0017A    93           PACK   PKB,B                  25 67 85                    330
   0000EA D205 B1E0 B204 0024A 0026E    94           MVC    PK,ZEROS               CLEARS PK                   340
   0000F0 D202 B1E2 B1DD 0024C 00247    95           MVC    PK+2(3),PKB            00 00 25 67 85 00           350
   0000F6 D100 B1E5 B1E4 0024F 0024E    96           MVN    PK+5(1),PK+4           00 00 25 67 85 0S           360
   0000FC 94F0 B1E4      0024E          97           NI     PK+4,X'F0'             00 00 25 67 80 0S           370
   000100 45A0 B0EA      00154          98           BAL    10,EDRT                EDITS PKB (EXTENDED)        380
   000104 D20C B182 B1F5 001EC 0025F    99           MVC    BOUT,WORK              B IN OUTPUT AREA            390
                                       100    * MULTIPLYING IN BINARY MODE                                     400
   00010A F872 B20E B1DA 00278 00244   101           ZAP    DOUBLE,PKA                                         410
   000110 4F60 B20E      00278         102           CVB    6,DOUBLE               A IN GPR 6                  420
   000114 F872 B20E B1DD 00278 00247   103           ZAP    DOUBLE,PKB                                         430
   00011A 4F50 B20E      00278         104           CVB    5,DOUBLE               B IN GPR 5                  440
   00011E 1C46                         105           MR     4,6                    ACTUALLY GPR 5 TIMES GPR 6  450
   000120 4E50 B20E      00278         106           CVD    5,DOUBLE               PRODUCT IS ONLY IN 5        460
                                       107    * THE FOLLOWING EDITS THE PRODUCT, -2,089,572,928. THE LARGEST POSITIVE  470
                                       108    * NUMBER IN A REGISTER IS 2,147,483,647 AND LARGEST NEGATIVE NUMBER IS   480
                                       109    *  -2,147,483,648                                                490
   000124 D205 B1E0 B210 0024A 0027A   110           MVC    PK,DOUBLE+2            02 08 95 72 92 80           500
   00012A 45A0 B0EA      00154         111           BAL    10,EDRT                EDITS PRODUCT               510
```

```
LOC      OBJECT CODE          ADDR1  ADDR2   STMT    SOURCE STATEMENT                                       FDOS CL3-9 11/01/73

00012E  D20E B1AE B1F5  00218  0025F   112         MVC    PROD,WORK                    PROD IN OUTPUT AREA        520
                                       113  *                                                                     530
                                       114         PUT    LISTER                                                  540
                                       119  ENDUP  CLOSE  CARD,LISTER                                             550
                                       128         EOJ                                                            560
                                       131  *                                  SUBROUTINE                         570
000154  D20E B1F5 B1E6  0025F  00250   132  EDRT   MVC    WORK,PAT                                                580
00015A  4110 B200               0026A  133         LA     1,WORK+11                    ADDRESS OF DECIMAL POINT   590
00015E  DF0E B1F5 B1E0  0025F  0024A   134         EDMK   WORK,PK                                                 600
000164  4780 B104              0016E   135         BNM    POS                                                     610
000168  0610                           136         BCTR   1,0                                                     620
00016A  9260 1000       00000          137         MVI    0(1),C'-'                    ADDRESS OF MINUS SIGN      630
00016E  07FA                           138  POS    BR     10                                                      640
                                       139  *                                  AREA DESIGNATIONS                  650
000170                                 140  IN     DS     0CL80                                                   660
000170                                 141  A      DS     ZL10                                                    670
00017A                                 142  B      DS     ZL10                                                    680
000184                                 143         DS     CL60                                                    690
                                       144  *                                                                     700
0001C0                                 145  OUTPUT DS     0CL132                                                  710
0001C0  4040404040404040               146         DC     15C' '                                                  720
0001CF  D4E4D3E3C9D7D3C9               147         DC     CL10'MULTIPLIER'                                        740
0001D9  4040404040404040               148         DC     20C' '                                                  750
0001ED  D4E4D3E3C9D7D3C9               149         DC     CL12'MULTIPLICAND'                                      770
0001F9  4040404040404040               150         DC     36C' '                                                  780
00021D  D7D9D6C4E4C3E3                 151         DC     CL7'PRODUCT'                                            800
000224  4040404040404040               152         DC     32C' '                                                  810
0001C0                                 153         ORG    OUTPUT                                                  811
0001C0                                 154         DS     CL11                                                    812
0001CB                                 155  AOUT   DS     CL14                         BBB,BBB,813.76             813
0001D9                                 156         DS     CL19                                                    814
0001EC                                 157  BOUT   DS     CL13                         BBB,BB2,567.8              815
0001F9                                 158         DS     CL31                                                    816
000218                                 159  PROD   DS     CL15                                                    817
000227                                 160         DS     CL29                                                    818
                                       161  *                                                                     820
000244                                 162  PKA    DS     PL3                                                     830
000247                                 163  PKB    DS     PL3                                                     840
00024A                                 164  PK     DS     PL6                                                     850
000250  4020206B2020206B               165  PAT    DC     X'4020206B2020206B2020214B202020'                       860
                                       166  *             B D D , D D D , D D ( . D D D                           870
00025F                                 167  WORK   DS     CL15                                                    880
00026E  00000000000C                   168  ZEROS  DC     PL6'0'                                                  890
000278                                 169  DOUBLE DS     D                                                       900
000068                                 170         END    ANFANG                                                  910
```

```
LOC    OBJECT CODE       ADDR1 ADDR2  STMT   SOURCE STATEMENT
000280 5B5BC2D6D7C5D540                171          =C'$$BOPEN '
000288 5B5BC2C3D3D6E2C5                172          =C'$$BCLOSE'
000290 00000038                        173          =A(LISTER)
000294 00000000                        174          =A(CARD)
```

FDOS CL3-9 11/01/73

MULTIPLIER   MULTIPLICAND   PRODUCT   ⟶ ANSWER

−813.76   2,567.8   −2,089,572.928

Program Eight

Binary Division with EDMK and Half-Adjustment

There are two new features in this program:

1. Instead of reading three cards in by means of three GET instructions, a BCT ("Branch on Count") is used to set up a loop. For an explanation, see the Appendix.
2. The answers were *half-adjusted* (rounded).

A flowchart for the first new feature is as follows:

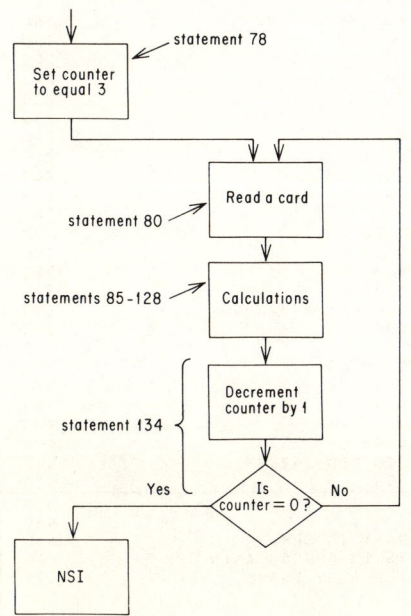

Note: The single BCT instruction takes care of the *decrement box* and the *decision box*.

Half-adjustment is accomplished by adding 05 or 50 to the proper byte of a positive number, or by subtracting 05 or 50 from the proper byte of a negative number. Assuming the number is in a register, the LTR instruction sets the condition code. The flowchart is as follows:

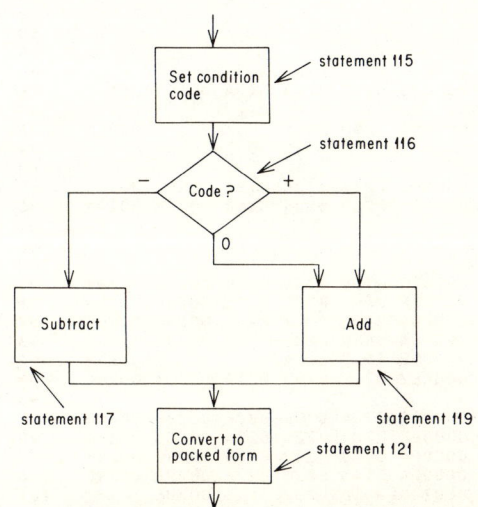

Binary division is not the most straightforward process in the world. It is explained in the Appendix. Steps 104 through 113 should be studied carefully.

The answers are shown on page 18.

Binary Division with EDMK and Half-Adjustment   45

```
// JOB EIGHT                                              17.53.22
* BINARY DIVISION WITH EDMARK AND HALF-ADJUSTMENT
// OPTION LINK                                                020
// EXEC ASSEMBLY                                              030
```

PAGE   1

```
   LOC  OBJECT CODE      ADDR1  ADDR2  STMT   SOURCE STATEMENT                             FDOS CL3-9 11/01/73
                                          1          PRINT NOGEN                                              040
  000000                                  2 EIGHT    START                                                    050
                                          3 *                             DTF SECTION                         060
                                          4 CARD     DTFCD DEVADDR=SYSRDR,IOAREA1=CRDIN,EOFADDR=FINIS          070
                                         25 PRINTER  DTFPR BLKSIZE=132,DEVADDR=SYSLST,IOAREA1=OUTPUT,CONTROL=YES 090
                                         46 *                             HOUSEKEEPING SECTION                110
  000068 05B0                             47 BEGIN   BALR  11,0                                               120
  00006A                                  48         USING *,11                                               130
                                          49         OPEN  CARD,PRINTER                                       140
                                         58 *                             PROCEDURE SECTION                   150
                                         59         CNTRL  PRINTER,SK,1          SKIP TO TOP OF PAGE          160
                                         65         PUT    PRINTER               HEADING                      170
                                         70         CNTRL  PRINTER,SP,2          SPACE TWO EXTRA LINES        180
  0000A6 D783 B18A B18A 001F4 001F4       76         XC     OUTPUT,OUTPUT                                     190
                                         77 * SET COUNTER TO PROCESS THREE INPUT CARDS                        200
  0000AC 4890 B256           002C0        78         LH    9,=H'3'                3 IN GPR 9                  210
                                         79 * READ A CARD AND PACK THE CONTENTS                               220
                                         80 AGAIN    GET   CARD                                               230
  0000BC F239 B226 B136 00290 001A0       85         PACK  PKA,A                  03 57 86 3+                 240
  0000C2 F239 B22A B140 00294 001AA       86         PACK  PKB,B                  02 47 99 3-                 250
                                         87 * PRE-EDIT AND EDMARK A. IT WOULD BE EASIER TO USE SEPARATE PATTERNS 260
                                         88 * FOR A, B AND C. THIS METHOD ILLUSTRATES THE POWER OF ASSEMBLER  270
                                         89 * CONTROL                                                         280
  0000C8 D704 B22E B22E 00298 00298       90         XC    PK,PK                  00 00 00 00 00              290
  0000CE D203 B22E B226 00298 00290       91         MVC   PK(4),PKA              03 57 86 3+ 00              300
  0000D4 D100 B232 B231 0029C 0029B       92         MVN   PK+4(1),PK+3           03 57 86 3+ 0+              310
  0000DA 94F0 B231      0029B             93         NI    PK+3,X'F0'             03 57 86 30 0+              320
  0000DE 45A0 B11A      00184             94         BAL   10,EDM                 EDITS A TO BB3,578.6300     330
  0000E2 D209 B197 B21A 00201 00284       95         MVC   AOUT,WORK              BB3,578.63                  340
                                         96 * PRE-EDIT AND EDMARK B.                                          350
  0000E8 D704 B22E B22E 00298 00298       97         XC    PK,PK                  00 00 00 00 00              360
  0000EE D203 B22E B22A 00298 00294       98         MVC   PK(4),PKB              02 47 99 3- 00              370
  0000F4 D100 B232 B231 0029C 0029B       99         MVN   PK+4(1),PK+3           02 47 99 3- 0-              380
  0000FA F143 B22E B22E 00298 00298      100         MVO   PK(5),PK(4)            00 24 79 93 --              390
  000100 940F B232      0029C            101         NI    PK+4,X'0F'             00 24 79 93 0-              400
  000104 45A0 B11A      00184            102         BAL   10,EDM                 EDITS B TO BBB-247.9930     410
  000108 D20A B1C3 B21A 0022D 00284      103         MVC   BOUT,WORK              BBB-247.993                 420
                                        104 * DIVIDEND INTO BINARY                                            430
  00010E F873 B236 B226 002A0 00290      105         ZAP   DOUBLE,PKA                                         440
  000114 4F40 B236      002A0            106         CVB   4,DOUBLE               A IN BINARY IN GPR 4        450
  000118 8E40 0020      00020            107         SRDA  4,32                   SIGN BITS IN GPR 4, A IN GPR 5 460
  00011C 5C40 B186      001F0            108         M     4,K                    MULTIPLIES A BY 10**6       470
                                        109 * DIVISOR INTO BINARY                                             480
  000120 F873 B236 B22A 002A0 00294      110         ZAP   DOUBLE,PKB                                         490
  000126 4F60 B236      002A0            111         CVB   6,DOUBLE               B IN BINARY IN GPR 6        500
```

```
LOC      OBJECT CODE           ADDR1  ADDR2  STMT    SOURCE STATEMENT                                        FDOS CL3-9 11/01/73

                                      112 * DIVIDE AND HALF-ADJUST                                                             510
00012A  1D46                          113          DR     4,6              QUOTIENT IN GPR 5, REMAIN-                          520
                                      114 *                                   DER IN GPR 4                                     530
00012C  1255                          115          LTR    5,5               TEST FOR SIGN                                      540
00012E  47B0 B0D0            0013A    116          BNM    PLUS              IF POSITIVE, BRANCH                                550
000132  4B50 B258            002C2    117          SH     5,=H'5'           IF NEGATIVE, SUBT 5 AND                            560
000136  47F0 B0D4            0013E    118          B      OUT               SKIP THE NEXT STEP                                 570
00013A  4A50 B258            002C2    119 PLUS     AH     5,=H'5'           IF POSITIVE, ADD 5                                 580
                                      120 * CONVERT TO PACKED DECIMAL AND EDMARK                                               590
00013E  4E50 B236            002A0    121 OUT      CVD    5,DOUBLE                     00 00 00 00 14 43 04 1-                 600
000142  D704 B22E B22E 00298 00298    122          XC     PK,PK                        00 00 00 00 00                          610
000148  D204 B22E B239 00298 002A3    123          MVC    PK,DOUBLE+3       00 14 43 04 1-                                     620
00014E  F143 B22E B22E 00298 00298    124          MVO    PK(5),PK(4)       00 01 44 30 4-                                     630
000154  45A0 B11A            00184    125          BAL    10,EDM            EDITS QUOT TO BBBB-14.4304                         640
000158  D20B B1EF B21A 00259 00284    126          MVC    QUOT,WORK         BBB-14.4304                                        650
                                      127 *                                                                                    660
                                      128          PUT    PRINTER                                                              670
                                      133 * REPEAT FOR THREE CARDS, THEN END                                                   680
00016A  4690 B046            000B0    134          BCT    9,AGAIN           DECREMENTS,THEN TESTS FOR                          690
                                      135 *                                    ZERO. IF ZERO, FALLS THRU.                      700
                                      136 FINIS    CLOSE  CARD,PRINTER                                                         705
                                      145          EOJ                                                                         710
                                      148 *                                           SUBROUTINE                               720
000184  D20B B21A B20E 00284 00278    149 EDM      MVC    WORK,PAT                                                             730
00018A  4110 B221            0028B    150          LA     1,WORK+7          ADDRESS OF DECIMAL POINT                           740
00018E  DF0B B21A B22E 00284 00298    151          EDMK   WORK,PK                                                              750
000194  47B0 B134            0019E    152          BNM    POS                                                                  760
000198  0610                          153          BCTR   1,0               ADDRESS OF MINUS SIGN                              770
00019A  9260 1000            00000    154          MVI    0(1),C'-'                                                            780
00019E  07FA                          155 POS      BR     10                                                                   790
                                      156 *                                           AREA DESIGNATIONS                        800
0001A0                                157 CRDIN    DS     0CL80                                                                810
0001A0                                158 A        DS     ZL10              3578.63                                            820
0001AA                                159 B        DS     ZL10              -247.993                                           830
0001B4                                160          DS     CL60                                                                 840
0001F0  000F4240                      161 K        DC     F'1000000'                                                           850
0001F4                                162 OUTPUT   DS     0CL132                                                               860
0001F4  4040404040404040              163          DC     15C' '                                                               870
000203  C4C9E5C9C4C5D5C4              164          DC     CL8'DIVIDEND'                                                        890
00020B  4040404040404040              165          DC     38C' '                                                               900
000231  C4C9E5C9E2D6D9                166          DC     CL7'DIVISOR'                                                         920
000238  4040404040404040              167          DC     37C' '                                                               930
00025D  D8E4D6E3C9C5D5E3              168          DC     CL8'QUOTIENT'                                                        950
000265  4040404040404040              169          DC     19C' '                                                               960
0001F4                                170          ORG    OUTPUT                                                               970
```

```
LOC      OBJECT CODE       ADDR1 ADDR2  STMT    SOURCE STATEMENT                                              FDOS CL3-9 11/01/73
0001F4                                   171           DS     CL13                                             971
000201                                   172  AOUT     DS     CL10                                             972
00020B                                   173           DS     CL34                                             973
00022D                                   174  BOUT     DS     CL11                                             974
000238                                   175           DS     CL33                                             975
000259                                   176  QUOT     DS     CL12              -14.430366                     976
000265                                   177           DS     CL19                                             977
                                         178  *                                                                978
000278  4020206B2020214B                 179  PAT      DC     X'4020206B2020214B20202020'                      980
                                         180  *               B DD,DD(.DDDD                                    990
000284                                   181  WORK     DS     CL12                                             1000
000290                                   182  PKA      DS     PL4                                              1010
000294                                   183  PKB      DS     PL4                                              1020
000298                                   184  PK       DS     PL5                                              1030
0002A0                                   185  DOUBLE   DS     D                                                1050
000068                                   186           END    BEGIN                                            1060
0002A8  5B5BC2D6D7C5D540                 187                  =C'$$BOPEN '
0002B0  5B5BC2C3D3D6E2C5                 188                  =C'$$BCLOSE'
0002B8  00000038                         189                  =A(PRINTER)
0002BC  00000000                         190                  =A(CARD)
0002C0  0003                             191                  =H'3'
0002C2  0005                             192                  =H'5'
```

DIVIDEND	DIVISOR	QUOTIENT
3,578.63	-247.993	-14.4304
-2,103.41	826.511	-2.5449
-8,364.24	-693.455	12.0617

} ANSWER

Program Nine

Simple Formula

The purpose of this program is displayed in statements 1-11.

There are three new features in this program:

1. A set of cards was read in by an unconditional branch (statement 126).
2. The ED (edit) command was used for intermediate results (statement 107).
3. Decimal arithmetic was used for the first time.

The ED instruction and the decimal instructions are explained in the Appendix.

The ED instruction is important chiefly for work not requiring a floating dollar sign or minus sign. It is not much simpler than the powerful EDMK instruction and is included here merely to demonstrate how it works.

Decimal arithmetic is much easier to code than binary, but is also slower in execution. If speed is an important factor in a program, numbers should be converted to binary, and binary arithmetic should be used. Otherwise, decimal arithmetic is perfectly satisfactory.

Notice that the print area was formed by a heading (beginning in statement 177), then an ORG was used (statement 187) to assign regions for the intermediate results, and another ORG (statement 201) to provide for the final answer. There can be a large number of ORG's to do this kind of thing, but the use of DC's to define constants can be used *only in the first area defined*. For this reason, the words

THE RESULT IS

had to be moved in. They are defined in statement 220 and moved in in statement 145.

In working this kind of problem, it is very important to *scale* results. This means that

a. the maximum length of each number must be estimated, and
b. the positions of the decimal points must be calculated.

Again, this is not the easiest matter in the world, but it is essential.

The answers are shown on page 53.

```
// JOB NINE                                   17.18.31
* SIMPLE FORMULA                                         010
// OPTION LINK                                           020
// EXEC ASSEMBLY                                         030
```

PAGE   1

```
   LOC    OBJECT CODE     ADDR1  ADDR2   STMT   SOURCE STATEMENT                                      FDOS CL3-9 11/01/73

                                           1 * THIS IS AN ILLUSTRATIVE PROGRAM TO READ N NUMBERS FROM CARDS, SQUARE      040
                                           2 * EACH NUMBER, FIND THE SUM AND DIVIDE BY N. INPUT IS IN THE FORM           050
                                           3 * (3).(1). AFTER SQUARING, THE MAXIMUM SIZE IS (6).(2). FOR UP TO TEN       060
                                           4 * CARDS, THE MAXIMUM SIZE IS (7).(2). AFTER DIVIDING, THE MAXIMUM           070
                                           5 * RESULT IS (6).(2).                                                        080
                                           6 *    IN THIS PROGRAM, THE INPUT CARDS CONTAIN 34.5, 61.3, 52.7, 81.9 AND    090
                                           7 * -127.2. THE SUM OF SQUARES IS 30,612.68. THE QUOTIENT IS 6,122.536        100
                                           8 * BEFORE HALF-ADJUSTMENT. THESE VALUES ARE FOR TESTING THE PROGRAM.         110
                                           9 *    IN ORDER TO PROVIDE 'BUS STOP' CHECKING, INTERMEDIATE RESULTS ARE      120
                                          10 * PRINTED AT SUITABLE INTERVALS. FOR A WORKING PROGRAM, THE FINAL           130
                                          11 * DEBUGGED PROGRAM WOULD HAVE ALL TEST CARDS REMOVED.                       140
                                          12 *                                                                           150
                                          13          PRINT NOGEN                                                        160
   000000                                 14 NINE     START                                                              170
                                          15 *                      DTF SECTION                                          180
                                          16 CARDF    DTFCD DEVADDR=SYSRDR,IOAREA1=CARD,EOFADDR=OVER                     190
                                          37 PRINTF   DTFPR BLKSIZE=132,DEVADDR=SYSLST,IOAREA1=PRINT,CONTROL=YES         200
                                          58 *                                                                           220
                                          59 *                 HOUSEKEEPING SECTION                                      230
   000068 05B0                            60 BEGIN    BALR  11,0                                                         240
                                          61          USING *,11                                                         250
   00006A                                 62          OPEN  CARDF,PRINTF                                                 260
                                          71 *                 PROCEDURE SECTION                                         270
                                          72 * SET UP 'PRINT' FOR INTERMEDIATE RESULTS. FOR DEBUGGING ONLY, IT WAS       280
                                          73 * NOT NECESSARY TO DO MORE THAN MINOR EDITING.                              290
                                          74          CNTRL PRINTF,SK,1              SKIP TO TOP OF PAGE                 300
                                          80          PUT   PRINTF                   HEADING FOR CHECK SHEET             310
                                          85          CNTRL PRINTF,SP,3              SPACE 3 EXTRA LINES                 320
   0000A6 D783 B162 B162 001CC 001CC      91          XC    PRINT,PRINT                                                  330
                                          92 * SET SUM AND COUNTER (N) TO ZERO                                           340
   0000AC F855 B1E6 B1EC 00250 00256      93          ZAP   SUM,ZEROS                00 00 00 00 00 0S                   350
   0000B2 F811 B1F2 B1F0 0025C 0025A      94          ZAP   N,ZEROS+4(2)             00 0S                               360
                                          95 * REGULAR PROCEDURE                                                         370
                                          96 AGAIN    GET   CARDF                    READS A AS XXXX ZONED               380
   0000C4 D209 B187 B112 001F1 0017C     101          MVC   AOUT,A                   A IN CHECK AREA, NOT EDITED         390
   0000CA F229 B1F4 B112 0025E 0017C     102          PACK  PKA,A                    0X XX XS                            400
   0000D0 F852 B1F7 B1F4 00261 0025E     103          ZAP   SQUARE,PKA               00 00 00 0X XX XS = A               410
   0000D6 FC52 B1F7 B1F4 00261 0025E     104          MP    SQUARE,PKA               00 0X XX XX XX XS = A*A             420
                                         105 * EDIT SQUARE FOR DISPLAY ONLY (NO DECIMAL POINTS)                          430
   0000DC D20D B198 B1FD 00202 00267     106          MVC   WORKS,PATS                                                   440
   0000E2 DE0D B198 B1F7 00202 00261     107          ED    WORKS,SQUARE                                                 450
                                         108 * REGULAR PROCEDURE                                                         460
   0000E8 FA55 B1E6 B1F7 00250 00261     109          AP    SUM,SQUARE               00 XX XX XX XX XS = MAXIMUM         470
                                         110 * EDIT SUM FOR DISPLAY ONLY (NO DECIMAL POINTS)                             480
   0000EE D20D B1BB B1FD 00225 00267     111          MVC   WORKA,PATS                                                   490
```

50

```
LOC      OBJECT CODE      ADDR1 ADDR2  STMT      SOURCE STATEMENT                              FDOS CL3-9 11/01/73

0000F4 DE0D B1BB B1E6    00225 00250   112             ED      WORKA,SUM                                            500
                                       113     * REGULAR PROCEDURE                                                  510
0000FA FA10 B1F2 B250    0025C 002BA   114             AP      N,=P'1'                      STEPS COUNTER           520
                                       115     * EDIT N FOR DISPLAY ONLY                                            530
000100 D203 B17B B20B    001E5 00275   116             MVC     WORKN,PATN                                           540
000106 DE03 B17B B1F2    001E5 0025C   117             ED      WORKN,N                                              550
                                       118     * PRINT INTERMEDIATE RESULTS - N, A, SQUARE, AND SUM                 560
                                       119     *                                                                    565
                                       120             PUT     PRINTF                                               570
                                       125     *                                                                    580
000118 47F0 B04E               00088   126             B       AGAIN                        REPEAT UNTIL /* IS REACHED,  590
                                       127     *                                            THEN GO TO EOFADDR = OVER    600
                                       128     * THE DP COMMAND FORMS, IN THE FIRST OPERAND, A COMPOSITE SUCH THAT THE   610
                                       129     * FIRST PART IS THE PACKED QUOTIENT AND THE SECOND PART IS THE PACKED    620
                                       130     * REMAINDER WITH LENGTH EQUAL TO THAT OF THE DIVISOR. IN THIS PROGRAM,   630
                                       131     * ALLOWING ONE PLACE FOR HALF-ADJUSTMENT, THE MAXIMUM QUOTIENT HAS THE   640
                                       132     * FORM (6).(3) OR 5 BYTES. THE MAXIMUM DIVISOR IS XX OR TWO BYTES.      650
                                       133     * THEREFORE, THE RESULT AREA IS DEFINED AS A 7-BYTE FIELD, WITH THE     660
                                       134     * FIRST 5 BYTES DEFINED AS THE QUOTIENT.                               670
                                       135     *                                                                    680
00011C F865 B20F B1E6    00279 00250   136     OVER    ZAP     RESULT,SUM                   00 00 XX XX XX XX XS    690
000122 FC61 B20F B24E    00279 002B8   137             MP      RESULT,=P'10'                TO PERMIT HALF-ADJUSTMENT 700
000128 FD61 B20F B1F2    00279 0025C   138             DP      RESULT,N                     XX XX XX XX 0S 0X XS    710
00012E FA40 B20F B251    00279 002BB   139             AP      QUOT,=P'5'                   HALF-ADJUSTS            720
                                       140     * EDIT QUOTIENT WHICH MUST BE POSITIVE IN THIS CASE                  730
                                       141     * ADJUST PAGE, THEN PRINT RESULT                                     760
000134 D783 B162 B162    001CC 001CC   142             XC      PRINT,PRINT                                          770
00013A D20B B197 B216    00201 00280   143             MVC     ANS,PATQ                                             740
000140 DE0B B197 B20F    00201 00279   144             ED      ANS,QUOT                                             750
000146 D20C B18A B222    001F4 0028C   145             MVC     RESOUT,RES                   MESSAGE                 ,//
                                       146             CNTRL   PRINTF,SP,3                  SPACE 3 EXTRA LINES     810
                                       152             PUT     PRINTF                                               820
                                       157     *                                                                    830
                                       158             CLOSE   CARDF,PRINTF                                         840
                                       167             EOJ                                                          850
                                       170     *                                            AREA DEFINITIONS        860
00017C                                 171     CARD    DS      0CL80                                                870
00017C                                 172     A       DS      ZL10                                                 880
000186                                 173             DS      CL70                                                 890
                                       174     *                                                                    900
0001CC                                 175     PRINT   DS      0CL132                                               910
                                       176     * HEADING                                                            920
0001CC 4040404040404040               177             DC      28C' '                                               925
0001E8 D5                              178             DC      C'N'                                                 930
0001E9 4040404040404040               179             DC      16C' '                                                935
```

```
LOC      OBJECT CODE      ADDR1 ADDR2    STMT        SOURCE STATEMENT                                            FDOS CL3-9 11/01/73

0001F9  C1                                180              DC      C'A'                                                              940
0001FA  4040404040404040                  181              DC      17C' '                                                            945
00020B  E2D8E4C1D9C5                      182              DC      C'SQUARE'                                                         950
000211  4040404040404040                  183              DC      31C' '                                                            955
000230  E2E4D4                            184              DC      C'SUM'                                                            960
000233  4040404040404040                  185              DC      29C' '                                                            965
                                          186         * TABLE                                                                        970
0001CC                                    187              ORG     PRINT                                                             975
0001CC                                    188              DS      CL25                                                              980
                                          189         * WORK AREA FOR N                                                              985
0001E5                                    190  WORKN       DS      ZL4                                                               990
0001E9                                    191              DS      CL8                                                               995
0001F1                                    192  AOUT        DS      ZL10                                                              1000
0001FB                                    193              DS      CL7                                                               1010
                                          194         * SQUARES                                                                      1015
000202                                    195  WORKS       DS      ZL14                                                              1020
000210                                    196              DS      CL21                                                              1025
                                          197         * PARTIAL SUMS                                                                 1030
000225                                    198  WORKA       DS      ZL14                                                              1035
000233                                    199              DS CL29                                                                   1040
                                          200         * MESSAGE                                                                      1045
0001CC                                    201              ORG     PRINT                                                             1050
0001CC                                    202              DS      CL40                                                              1100
0001F4                                    203  RESOUT      DS      CL13                                                              1105
000201                                    204  ANS         DS      CL12                                                              1110
00020D                                    205              DS      CL67                                                              1115
                                          206         *                                                                              
000250                                    207  SUM         DS      PL6                                                               1120
000256  00000000000C                      208  ZEROS       DC      PL6'0'              00 00 00 00 00 0S                             1130
00025C                                    209  N           DS      PL2                                                               1140
00025E                                    210  PKA         DS      PL3                                                               1150
000261                                    211  SQUARE      DS      PL6                                                               1160
000267  4020202020202020                  212  PATS        DC      XL14'40202020202020202020202020204060'                             1170
                                          213         *                B D D D D D D D D D D D B -                                   1180
000275  40202021                          214  PATN        DC      XL4'40202021'                                                     1190
                                          215         *              B D D (                                                         1200
000279                                    216  QUOT        DS      0PL5                                                              1210
000279                                    217  RESULT      DS      PL7                                                               1220
000280  402020206B202021                  218  PATQ        DC      XL12'402020206B2020214B202040'                                    1230
                                          219         *              B D D D , D D ( . D D B                                         1240
00028C  E3C8C540D9C5E2E4                  220  RES         DC      CL13'THE RESULT IS'                                               1245
000068                                    221              END     BEGIN                                                             1250
0002A0  5B5BC2D6D7C5D540                  222                      =C'$$BOPEN '
0002A8  5B5BC2C3D3D6E2C5                  223                      =C'$$BCLOSE'
0002B0  00000038                          224                      =A(PRINTF)
```

```
LOC      OBJECT CODE    ADDR1 ADDR2  STMT    SOURCE STATEMENT
0002B4   00000000                    225             =A(CARDF)
0002B8   010C                        226             =P'10'
0002BA   1C                          227             =P'1'
0002BB   5C                          228             =P'5'
```

```
        N           A           SQUARE              SUM

        1          345          119025             119025
        2          613          375769             494794
        3          527          277729             772523
        4          819          670761            1443284
        5          127K        1617984            3061268
```
} INTERMEDIATE RESULTS (PARTLY EDITED)

```
              THE RESULT IS   6,122.54
```
} ANSWER

Program Ten

Use of Tape for Scratch

One of the problems that often faces a programmer is *storage limitations*, especially in commercial and industrial applications. It is easy enough to run out of core if the program is very large and/or the amount of data is very large. In such a case, supplementary storage on tape, disk, drum, etc. is required.

In this program, 9 cards with data on them were read into core, one at a time, and transferred to tape for temporary storage, then processed (90,000 cards, a more realistic situation, would obscure the points being made). This is often called using the supplementary storage for "scratch," i.e., like a scratch-pad. There are many new features to be explained:

1. There is an *assignment* card, the third card, among the job control cards. (Note the spelling.) At this installation, one of the tape drives has the physical number 180$_x$ and the logical system number SYS004. At other installations, the machine number and the system number may or may not be these.
2. Note that the ESD has an extra module to handle the tape.
3. The tape is going to be used both for input and for output. Therefore, *two* file definitions are needed, one for input and one for output. These are explained separately in (4) and (5).
4. Statement 27 defines the output file. It is essential to understand the standard I/O programming convention that the programmer must consider that he is sitting within the *core* of the machine. Then, if data goes from core to tape, this is *output*. If data goes from tape to core, it is *input*. BLKSIZE=80 tells the computer that it is to read 80 bytes at a time (these are card images, in this program). The ASSGN job control card must agree with DEVADDR=SYS004. FILABL=NO means that the programmer is not labeling the file (it is just being used temporarily for scratch). IOAREA1=CARDIN tells the computer where, in core, the data is coming from, in order to be copied to tape. TYPEFLE=OUTPUT designates this as an output file. Notice the X at the end of the first line of statement 27. This X is in card column 72 and is called a *continuation symbol*. If there is too much information to be placed on one card, the information may be continued onto one or more additional cards provided there is a symbol in cc 72. There are other possible options in the DTF for magnetic tape. For these, see the appropriate manual.
5. Statement 58 defines the input file. It is not necessary to write TYPEFLE=INPUT because this is understood by default if not written. However, for input files it is always necessary to tell what to do when there are no more input records. This is at the instruction called TPEND (statement 203). The other options are self-explanatory.

6. The files are opened in statement 116 and, in statements 144-154, all the cards are read into CARDIN then copied onto the tape.
7. In statement 156, the two files no longer needed are closed.
8. In statement 165, the tape is rewound so that the beginning of the tape is again under the reading and writing head. In some installations, the REWIND is automatic and need not be specified.
9. In statement 172, the tape file is opened again but, this time, it is an input file, meaning that it will be used to bring data into core.
10. Statements 180 through 201 get the information into core, card by card, and edit. Each line is printed separately.
11. Statement 203 closes the files.
12. On page 60, note the job control card:

// PAUSE MOUNT TAPE ON X'180' FOR SCRATCH

This card alternatively could have been put at the beginning of the program with the other job control cards. At any point of occurrence of pause, the computer stops and the message is printed for the console operator. This person then prepares the proper tape drive, activates it, then presses EOB ("end of block") at the console. The program can then proceed.

13. In this program, it was assumed that the usual commercial output was desired. For this reason, statements 186 through 190 provided for a floating dollar sign, and the pattern (statement 242) allowed for the suffix CR where there was a balance ("credit") instead of an amount owed ("debit").

The results are shown on page 61.

```
        // JOB TEN                                              19.13.13
        *  USE OF TAPE FOR SCRATCH.
    ──▶ // ASSGN SYS004,X'180'                                      020
        // OPTION LINK                                              030
        // EXEC ASSEMBLY                                            040
```

                                EXTERNAL SYMBOL DICTIONARY   PAGE   1

```
SYMBOL    TYPE ID  ADDR   LENGTH LD ID

TEN       SD   01  000000 000388
IJCFZIZ0  ER   02
IJFFZZZZ  ER   03
IJDFCZZZ  ER   04
```

CROSS-REFERENCE

```
SYMBOL     LEN    VALUE   DEFN     REFERENCES
AGAIN      C0004  000162  00146    0154
AMT        C0010  0002A0  00221    0185
AMTOUT     C0018  000308  00239    0195
CARDF      C0006  000000  00009    0122  0146  0162  0250
CARDIN     C0080  000214  00216    0020  0022  0050  0051  0052  0054
CDEND      C0004  000180  00159    0021
CODE       C0004  000282  00219    0194
CODOUT     C0004  0002E6  00237    0194
IJCX0001   C0008  000020  00022    0012
IJF10002   C0008  00C070  00050    0033
IJF10003   C0008  0000C8  00081    0064
IJF20002   C0004  00007C  00052
IJF20003   C0004  0000D4  00083
IJJC0011   C0004  000184  00161
IJJC0016   C0004  000204  00208
IJJ00005   C0004  000128  00121
IJJ00013   C0004  0001A4  00177
IJJZ0001   C0001  000032  00026
IJJZ0004   C0001  000120  00112
INTAPE     C0006  000090  00061    0178  0182  0209  0252
NAME       C0030  000264  00218    0193
NAMOUT     C0030  0002BE  00235    0193
OUTTAPE    C0006  00C038  00030    0123  0151  0163  0167  0251
OVER       C0004  0001AE  00182    0201
PAT        C0018  000338  00242    0186
PK         00006  00035C  00245    0185  0188
PRINT      00132  000284  00224    0106  0111  0192  0192  0233
PRINTF     00006  0000F0  00095    0124  0128  0134  0139  0198  0210  0249
START      C0002  000120  00114    0246
TEN        C0001  000000  00004
TPEND      C0004  000200  00206    0076
TPIN       00080  000264  00217    0081  0082
WORK       C0018  00034A  00244    0186  0187  0188  0195
```

PAGE 1

11/05/73

NO STATEMENTS FLAGGED IN THIS ASSEMBLY

JOB TEN   11/05/73   DISK LINKAGE EDITOR DIAGNOSTIC OF INPUT

```
ACTION TAKEN   MAP
LIST    AUTOLINK    IJCFZIZ0
LIST    AUTOLINK    IJDFCZZZ
LIST    AUTOLINK    IJFFZZZZ
LIST    ENTRY
```

```
LOC     OBJECT CODE      ADDR1  ADDR2  STMT    SOURCE STATEMENT                               FDOS CL3-9 11/05/73

                                          1  * THE PURPOSE OF THIS PROGRAM IS TO READ CARDS TO TAPE, THEN PRINT    050
                                          2  * THE INFORMATION IN EDITED FORM.                                    60
                                          3            PRINT  NOGEN                                               61
000000                                    4  TEN       START                                          CONTINUATION 62
                                          5  *                          DTF SECTION                   SYMBOL       70
                                          6  CARDF     DTFCD  DEVADDR=SYSRDR,IOAREA1=CARDIN,EOFADDR=CDEND          080
                                         27  OUTTAPE   DTFMT  BLKSIZE=80,DEVADDR=SYS004,FILABL=NO,IOAREA1=CARDIN,TYPE(X) 110
                                                             LE=OUTPUT                                             120
                                         58  INTAPE    DTFMT  BLKSIZE=80,DEVADDR=SYS004,EOFADDR=TPEND,FILABL=NO,IOAREAX 140
                                                             1=TPIN                                                150
                                         92  PRINTF    DTFPR  BLKSIZE=132,DEVADDR=SYSLST,IOAREA1=PRINT,CONTROL=YES 170
                                        113  *                          HOUSEKEEPING SECTION                      190
000120 05B0                             114  START     BALR   11,0                                                200
000122                                  115            USING  *,11                                                210
                                        116            OPEN   CARDF,OUTTAPE,PRINTF                                220
                                        126            CNTRL  PRINTF,SK,1         SKIP TO TOP OF PAGE             230
                                        132            PUT    PRINTF              PRINTS HEADING                  240
                                        137            CNTRL  PRINTF,SP,3         SKIPS 3 EXTRA LINES             250
                                        143  *                          PROCEDURE SECTION                         260
                                        144  AGAIN     GET    CARDF               DATA IN CARDIN                  270
                                        149            PUT    OUTTAPE             FROM CARDIN TO TAPE             280
00017A 47F0 B040                 00162  154            B      AGAIN               REPEATS UNTIL /* IS REACHED     290
                                        155  *                                                                   300
                                        156  CDEND     CLOSE  CARDF,OUTTAPE                                       310
                                        165            CNTRL  OUTTAPE,REW         REWIND TAPE                     320
                                        171  *                                                                   330
                                        172            OPEN   INTAPE                                              340
                                        180  OVER      GET    INTAPE              READS INTO TPIN                 350
0001BA F259 B23A B17E 0035C      002A0  185            PACK   PK,AMT              XX XX XX XX XX XS               360
0001C0 D211 B228 B216 0034A      00338  186            MVC    WORK,PAT            PREPARATION FOR EDITING         370
0001C6 4110 B234                 00356  187            LA     1,WORK+12           ADDRESS OF DECIMAL POINT        380
0001CA DF11 B228 B23A 0034A      0035C  188            EDMK   WORK,PK                                             390
0001D0 0610                             189            BCTR   1,0                                                 400
0001D2 925B 1000                 00000  190            MVI    0(1),C'$'           PLACES DOLLAR SIGN              410
                                        191  *                                                                   420
0001D6 D783 B192 B192 002B4      002B4  192            XC     PRINT,PRINT                                         430
0001DC D21D B19C B142 002BE      00264  193            MVC    NAMOUT,NAME                                         440
0001E2 D203 B1C4 B160 002E6      00282  194            MVC    CODOUT,CODE                                         450
0001E8 D211 B1E6 B228 00308      0034A  195            MVC    AMTOUT,WORK                                         460
                                        196            PUT    PRINTF              PRINTS ONE LINE                 470
0001FA 47F0 B08C                 001AE  201            B      OVER                                                480
                                        202  *                                                                   490
                                        203  TPEND     CLOSE  INTAPE,PRINTF                                       500
                                        212            EOJ                                                        510
                                        215  *                          AREA DESIGNATIONS                        520
000214                                  216  CARDIN    DS     CL80                                                530
000264                                  217  TPIN      DS     0CL80                                               540
000264                                  218  NAME      DS     CL30                                                550
000282                                  219  CODE      DS     XL4                                                 560
000286                                  220            DS     CL26                                                570
0002A0                                  221  AMT       DS     ZL10                                                580
```

```
                                                                                      PAGE    2

LOC     OBJECT CODE      ADDR1 ADDR2   STMT    SOURCE STATEMENT                 FDOS CL3-9 11/05/73

0002AA                                  222           DS      CL10                         590
                                        223    *                                           600
0002B4                                  224    PRINT  DS      0CL132                       610
0002B4  4040404040404040                225           DC      10C' '                       610
0002BE  D5C1D4C5                        226           DC      CL4'NAME'                    630
0002C2  4040404040404040                227           DC      36C' '                       640
0002E6  C3D6C4C5                        228           DC      CL4'CODE'                    660
0002EA  4040404040404040                229           DC      38C' '                       670
000310  C1D4D6E4D5E3                    230           DC      CL6'AMOUNT'                  690
000316  4040404040404040                231           DC      33C' '                       700
                                        232    *                                           701
0002B4                                  233           ORG     PRINT                        702
0002B4                                  234           DS      CL10                         703
0002BE                                  235    NAMOUT DS      CL30                         704
0002DC                                  236           DS      CL10                         705
0002E6                                  237    CODOUT DS      XL4                          706
0002EA                                  238           DS      CL30                         707
000308                                  239    AMTOUT DS      CL18                         708
00031A                                  240           DS      CL30                         709
                                        241    *                                           710
000338  402020206B202020             →  242    PAT    DC      X'402020206B2020206B2020214B202040C3D9'   730
                                        243    *                   B D D D , D D D , D D ( . D D B C R      740
00034A                                  244    WORK   DS      CL18                         750
00035C                                  245    PK     DS      PL6                          760
000120                                  246           END     START                        770
000368  5B5BC2D6D7C5D540                247                   =C'$$BOPEN '
000370  5B5BC2C3D3D6E2C5                248                   =C'$$BCLOSE'
000378  000000F0                        249                   =A(PRINTF)
00037C  00000000                        250                   =A(CARDF)
000380  00C00038                        251                   =A(OUTTAPE)
000384  00000090                        252                   =A(INTAPE)
```

```
11/05/73   PHASE   XFR-AD   LOCORE   HICORE   DSK-AD    ESD TYPE   LABEL      LOADED   REL-FR
           PHASE***  002920   002800   002EEF   5C 02 1  CSECT      TEN        002800   002800
                                                         CSECT      IJCFZIZO   002B88   002B88
                                                         CSECT      IJFFZZZZ   002C40   002C40
                                                         CSECT      IJDFCZZZ   002BF0   002BF0
                                                         *  ENTRY   IJDFZZZZ   002BF0
```

→ // PAUSE MOUNT TAPE ON X '180' FOR SCRATCH   800
  // EXEC   810

NAME	CODE	AMOUNT
SMOOT,ALEX	FB47	$.00
HENDERSON,FRANK	3S75	$158,629.24 CR
HENDERSON,FRANK B	3S23	$35,721.89
BAND,ALEXANDER	7P18	$635.93 CR
COMENIUS,ALBERT	AB23	$3,572.68 CR
SMITH,JOHN	FF23	$237.82 CR
SMYTH,SAMUEL	FA23	$2,375.18
SMITHSON,HENRY	EB25	$534.07
SMYTHE,GEORGE	1323	$1,000.00

Program Eleven

Use of Scratch Disk (WORKA Method)

The purpose of this program is explained in statements 1 through 4 on page 65. In this case, the data were read sequentially onto a disk, then back into core where it was printed as a table. The new features are explained in the following. This program used the *work-area method;* the next program, Program TWELVE, accomplishes the same purpose by another method.

1. // ASSGN SYS007,X'192' identifies the magnetic disk drive symbolic name and the machine number for this installation. It may or may not be the same in another installation.
2. Items 2 and 3 describe the job control statements for input and output files. It is fair to say that these may be slightly different for other installations. Consult the Computer Director (not the IBM manual). The next *pair* of instructions is used for the input disk.

// DLBL DSKIN,'FILE',01/001

defines a label for the input file as follows: DSKIN is the file name as given in statement 80, FILE is a symbolic name needed by the computer but not used in the program itself, and 01/001 is a symbol used in this installation to mean that this is a scratch file. It is actually the file expiration date in julian format. If this number is omitted, the file is "protected" and the next person to use it has to start at another place on the disk. The computer center supplies the information for its own installation.

// EXTENT SYS007,111111,,,1,9

describes the specific disk area. SYS007 agrees with the ASSGN. The number 111111 is the identification number of the scratch disk pack used at this installation. The computer center must be asked what the number of the scratch disk pack is. The parameters ,,,1,9 are required at this installation to tell where the information is to go on the disk.

3. The next *pair* of instructions is used for the output disk. Except for the file name, it is the same as (2). The purpose of the name, FILE, is to notify the computer that the same physical disk area is being used for input and output.
4. Note the PAUSE (for the console operator).
5. Statement 30. This is the definition of the output sequential disk file. Notice that the card image has only 80 bytes, but 8 extra bytes are needed for each card for the internal use of the computer (to keep count). In statement 248, the corresponding I/O area has 88 bytes to match. The high-order eight bytes are the ones used by IOCS (input-output control system) so that the useful information begins at OUT+8, a fact needed in statement 185.
6. Statement 80 defines the input file. The keyword parameter entries are as follows:

BLKSIZE=80	This is the size of the entire image of each card
RECSIZE=16	Each record has only 16 bytes. In other words, only part of the block is used in the program.
WORKA=YES	A work area will be used. This work area is LOGREC shown in statements 252-254.
RECFORM=FIXBLK	All records are the same fixed size.

7. Statements 180 through 191 read all the cards and enter them sequentially on the output disk. Note, in statement 185, that the 80 bytes of the cards are moved into OUT+8 for the reasons explained in (5).
8. After all the card images are on the disk, the two files no longer needed are closed. This is done in statement 193.
9. In statements 212 through 231, each card image is retrieved from the disk and the 16-byte record is placed in the work area (LOGREC). From there, it is printed.
10. Note statements 247 and 250. These ensure that I/O areas for disks will begin on a halfword boundary, i.e., an address divisible by 2. This is an engineering requirement.

The results of this program are shown on page 68.

```
// JOB ELEVEN                                                    19.16.57
* USE OF SCRATCH DISK (WORKA METHOD)
// ASSGN SYS007,X'192'                                           020
// DLBL DSKIN,'FILE',01/001                                      030
// EXTENT SYS007,111111,,,1,9                                    040
// DLBL DSKOUT,'FILE',01/001                                     050
// EXTENT SYS007,111111,,,1,9                                    055
// PAUSE PLEASE MOUNT SCRATCH DISK ON X'192', THEN PRESS EOB     056
// OPTION LINK                                                   060
// EXEC ASSEMBLY                                                 070
```

EXTERNAL SYMBOL DICTIONARY   PAGE   1

```
SYMBOL    TYPE ID   ADDR   LENGTH LD ID

ELEVEN     SD   01  000000 00041C
IJCFZIZ0   ER   02
IJGF0ZZZ   ER   03
IJGFIZZZ   ER   04
IJDFCZZZ   ER   05
```

```
LOC      OBJECT CODE       ADDR1  ADDR2   STMT    SOURCE STATEMENT                                                    FDOS CL3-9  11/05/73

                                             1  * THE PURPOSE OF THIS PROGRAM IS TO READ 4 CARDS ONTO A SCRATCH DISK,           080
                                             2  * THEN RETRIEVE THE INFORMATION AND PRINT A TABLE. IN THIS ILLUSTRATION         090
                                             3  * THE DATA ARE THE NAMES OF 20 CITIES AND THE AVERAGE TEMPERATURES OVER         100
                                             4  * A 30-YEAR PERIOD.                                                             110
                                             5  *                                                                               120
                                             6           PRINT  NOGEN                                                           130
000000                                       7  ELEVEN   START                                                                  140
                                             8  *                                  DTF SECTION                                  150
                                             9  CARDF    DTFCD  DEVADDR=SYSRDR,IOAREA1=CARDIN,EOFADDR=CDEND                     160
                                        → 30  DSKOUT   DTFSD  BLKSIZE=88,IOAREA1=OUT,TYPEFLE=OUTPUT                             170
                                        → 80  DSKIN    DTFSD  BLKSIZE=80,IOAREA1=IN,EOFADDR=DSKEND,                  *          180
                                                                RECSIZE=16,WORKA=YES,RECFORM=FIXBLK                              185
                                           125  PRINTF   DTFPR  DEVADDR=SYSLST,BLKSIZE=132,IOAREA1=PRINT,CONTROL=YES             190
                                           146  *                                  HOUSEKEEPING SECTION                         200
000190 05B0                                147  START    BALR   11,0                                                            210
000192                                     148           USING  *,11                                                            220
                                           149           OPEN   CARDF,DSKOUT,PRINTF                                             230
                                           159  * HEADING.                                                                      240
                                           160           CNTRL  PRINTF,SK,1   SKIP TO TOP OF PAGE                               250
                                           166           PUT    PRINTF        PRINT HEADING                                     260
                                           171           CNTRL  PRINTF,SP,3   SPACE 3 EXTRA LINES                               270
0001D2 D783 B1E2 B1E2 00374 00374          177           XC     PRINT,PRINT   CLEAN PRINT AREA                                  280
                                           178  *                                  PROCEDURE SECTION                            290
                                           179  * WRITE DATA ON SCRATCH DISK.                                                   300
                                           180  AGAIN    GET    CARDF                                                           310
0001E4 D24F B132 B0DA 002C4 0026C  → 185           MVC    OUT+8(80),CARDIN  THE FIRST 8 CC OF OUT ARE FOR IOCS                  320
                                           186           PUT    DSKOUT            ONE CARD IMAGE GOES TO THE DISK               330
0001F6 47F0 B046            001D8          191           B      AGAIN             CONTINUES UNTIL /* IS REACHED                 340
                                           192  *                                                                               350
                                        → 193  CDEND    CLOSE  DSKOUT,CARDF      AN END-OF-FILE IS MARKED ON THE               360
                                           202  *                                  DISK BECAUSE OF THE CLOSE                    370
                                           203           OPEN   DSKIN                                                           380
                                           211  *                                                                               390
                                           212  MORE     GET    DSKIN,LOGREC                                                    400
00022E D20A B215 B1D2 003A7 00364          218           MVC    NAME,N                                                          410
000234 D204 B229 B1DD 003BB 0036F          219           MVC    TEMP,T                                                          420
                                           220           PUT    PRINTF                                                          430
                                           225           CNTRL  PRINTF,SP,1                                                     440
000254 47F0 B08C            0021E          231           B      MORE              CONTINUES UNTIL END OF FILE                   450
                                           232  *                                                                               460
                                           233  DSKEND   CLOSE  DSKIN,PRINTF                                                    470
                                           242           EOJ                                                                    480
                                           245  *                                  AREA DESIGNATIONS                            490
00026C                                     246  CARDIN   DS     CL80                                                            500
0002BC                                   → 247           DS     0H
0002BC                                   → 248  OUT      DS     CL88   INCLUDES 8 BYTES FOR IOCS                                510
                                           249  *                                                                               520
                                         → 250           DS     0H                                                              521
000314                                     251  IN       DS     CL80                                                            522
000364                                   → 252  LOGREC   DS     0CL16                                                           530
000364                                     253  N        DS     CL11                                                            540
```

```
LOC      OBJECT CODE        ADDR1 ADDR2  STMT   SOURCE STATEMENT
00036F                                    254 T        DS    CL5                          550
                                          255 *                                           560
000374                                    256 PRINT    DS    OCL132                       570
                                          257 * HEADING.                                  580
000374   4040404040404040                 258          DC    50C' '                       590
0003A6   D5C1D4C540D6C640                 259          DC    CL12'NAME OF CITY'           600
0003B2   40404040404040                   260          DC    7C' '                        610
0003B9   C1E54B40E3C5D4D7                 261          DC    CL9'AV. TEMP.'               620
0003C2   4040404040404040                 262          DC    54C' '                       630
                                          263 * SPACES FOR PRINTOUT.                     640
000374                                    264          ORG   PRINT                        650
000374                                    265          DS    CL51                         660
0003A7                                    266 NAME     DS    CL11                         670
0003B2                                    267          DS    CL9                          680
0003BB                                    268 TEMP     DS    CL5                          690
0003C0                                    269          DS    CL56                         700
                                          270 *                                           710
000190                                    271          END   START                        720
0003F8   5B5BC2D6D7C5D540                 272                =C'$$BOPEN '
000400   5B5BC2C3D3D6E2C5                 273                =C'$$BCLOSE'
000408   00000160                         274                =A(PRINTF)
00040C   00000000                         275                =A(CARDF)
000410   00000038                         276                =A(DSKOUT)
000414   000000D8                         277                =A(DSKIN)
000418   00000364                         278                =A(LOGREC)
```

PAGE 2

FDOS CL3-9 11/05/73

CROSS-REFERENCE

```
SYMBOL      LEN   VALUE  DEFN    REFERENCES

AGAIN       00004 0001D8 00182   0191
CARDF       00006 000000 00012   0155  0182  0200  0275
CARDIN      C0080 00026C 00246   0023  0025  0185
CDEND       00004 0001FC 00196   0024
DSKEND      00004 000258 00236   0107
DSKIN       00006 000008 00083   0209  0214  0239  0277
DSKINS      00001 000112 00104
DSKOUT      00006 000038 00033   0156  0188  0199  0276
DSKOUTS     00001 000072 00054   0076
ELEVEN      00001 000000 00007
IJCX0001    00008 000020 00025   0015
IJGC0002    00008 0000A0 00072   0036
IJGC0003    00008 000140 00120   0086
IJJC0011    00004 000200 00198
IJJC0016    00004 00025C 00238
IJJO0005    00004 000198 00154
IJJO0012    00004 000214 00208
IJJZ0001    00001 000032 00029
IJJZ0002    00001 000008 00079
IJJZ0003    00001 000160 00124
IJJZ0004    00001 000190 00145
IN          C0080 000314 00251   0100  0115  0117  0123
LOGREC      C0016 000364 00252   0215  0278
MORE        00004 00021E 00214   0231
N           00011 000364 00253   0218
NAME        C0011 0003A7 00266   0218
OUT         00088 0002BC 00248   0050  0067  0069  0075  0185
PRINT       00132 000374 00256   0139  0144  0177  0177  0264
PRINTF      00006 000160 00128   0157  0162  0168  0173  0222  0227  0240  0274
START       00002 000190 00147   0271
T           00005 00036F 00254   0219
TEMP        00005 0003BB 00268   0219
```

NO STATEMENTS FLAGGED IN THIS ASSEMBLY

```
11/05/73   PHASE    XFR-AD  LOCORE  HICORE  DSK-AD    ESD TYPE  LABEL     LOADED  REL-FR

           PHASE*** 002990  002800  0030F5  5C 02 1   CSECT     ELEVEN    002800  002800
                                                      CSECT     IJCFZIZO  002C20  002C20
                                                      CSECT     IJGFOZZZ  002EB0  002EB0
                                                      CSECT     IJGFIZZZ  002CD8  002CD8
                                                      CSECT     IJDFCZZZ  002C88  002C88
                                                      *  ENTRY  IJDFZZZZ  002C88
```

NAME OF CITY	AV. TEMP.
ATLANTA	47.6
BALTIMORE	57.6
BOSTON	51.4
CHICAGO	50.8
COLUMBUS	52.0
DALLAS	65.8
DENVER	49.5
DETROIT	50.1
HARTFORD	49.9
HONOLULU	75.9
LOS ANGELES	64.4
MEMPHIS	61.5
MIAMI	75.1
NEW ORLEANS	69.4
NEW YORK	54.5
PHILA.	53.5
ST. LOUIS	55.3
SALT LAKE	50.9
SAN JUAN	78.3
WASH.,D.C.	57.0

Program Twelve

Use of Scratch Disk (IOREG Method)

This program illustrates another method of doing the same thing as Program ELEVEN. The advantage of this method is that it may save space in core, owing to the use of a *dummy section*. The following explains only the instructions different from ELEVEN.

1. In statement 80, IOREG=(12) identifies register 12 as the register to be used by the computer. Any available register between 2 and 12 may be used as an IOREG. IOCS automatically puts the address of input or output data in this register. In this specific case, the data are input.
2. Statement 149 tells Assembler that register 12 is to be used as the base register for the dummy section, LOGREC.
3. Every time statement 213 is reached, the address in register 12 is adjusted by IOCS.
4. Statement 268 identifies LOGREC as a DSECT (dummy section). This can be thought of as a section which is planned but which takes no space in core. In this program, there was no advantage because the amount of core used was so small, but in a very large program, the use of DSECTs is very valuable for the conservation of core space. As usual, there is a "trade-off" of core space vs. registers. In other words, if the programmer is short of space but doesn't need the register, a DSECT is a good idea. Otherwise, it is not. The method used here is sometimes called *symbolic addressing*.

```
// JOB TWELVE                                                        18.05.08
* USE OF SCRATCH DISK (IOREG METHOD).
// ASSGN SYS007,X'192'                                               020
// DLBL DSKIN,'FILE',01/001                                          030
// EXTENT SYS007,111111,,,1,9                                        040
// DLBL DSKOUT,'FILE',01/001                                         050
// EXTENT SYS007,111111,,,1,9                                        055
// PAUSE PLEASE MOUNT SCRATCH DISK ON X'192', THEN PRESS EOB         056
// OPTION LINK                                                       060
// EXEC ASSEMBLY                                                     070
```

```
  LOC   OBJECT CODE     ADDR1 ADDR2   STMT   SOURCE STATEMENT                                      FDOS CL3-9 11/01/73

                                         1  * THE PURPOSE OF THIS PROGRAM IS TO READ 4 CARDS ONTO A SCRATCH DISK,    080
                                         2  * THEN RETRIEVE THE INFORMATION AND PRINT A TABLE. IN THIS ILLUSTRATION  090
                                         3  * THE DATA ARE THE NAMES OF 20 CITIES AND THE AVERAGE TEMPERATURES OVER  100
                                         4  * A 30-YEAR PERIOD. THIS IS ANOTHER WAY. COMPARE WITH PROGRAM ELEVEN.    110
                                         5  *                                                                       120
                                         6           PRINT NOGEN                                                    130
 000000                                  7  TWELVE   START                                                          140
                                         8  *                            DTF SECTION                                150
                                         9  CARDF    DTFCD DEVADDR=SYSRDR,IOAREA1=CARDIN,EOFADDR=CDEND              160
                                        30  DSKOUT   DTFSD BLKSIZE=88,IOAREA1=OUT,TYPEFLE=OUTPUT                    170
                                        80  DSKIN    DTFSD BLKSIZE=80,IOAREA1=IN,EOFADDR=DSKEND,                 *  180
                                                           RECSIZE=16,IOREG=(12),RECFORM=FIXBLK                     185
                                       125  PRINTF   DTFPR DEVADDR=SYSLST,BLKSIZE=132,IOAREA1=PRINT,CONTROL=YES     190
                                       146  *                            HOUSEKEEPING SECTION                       200
 000190 05B0                           147  START    BALR  11,0                                                     210
 000192                                148           USING *,11                                                     220
 000000                                149           USING LOGREC,12                                                225
                                       150           OPEN  CARDF,DSKOUT,PRINTF                                      230
                                       160  * HEADING.                                                              240
                                       161           CNTRL PRINTF,SK,1    SKIP TO TOP OF PAGE                       250
                                       167           PUT   PRINTF         PRINT HEADING                             260
                                       172           CNTRL PRINTF,SP,3    SPACE 3 EXTRA LINES                       270
 0001D2 D783 B1CE B1CE 00360 00360     178           XC    PRINT,PRINT    CLEAN PRINT AREA                          280
                                       179  *                            PROCEDURE SECTION                          290
                                       180  * WRITE DATA ON SCRATCH DISK.                                           300
                                       181  AGAIN    GET   CARDF                                                    310
 0001E4 D24F B12E B0D6 002C0 00268     186           MVC   OUT+8(80),CARDIN  THE FIRST 8 CC OF OUT ARE FOR IOCS     320
                                       187           PUT   DSKOUT            ONE CARD IMAGE GOES TO THE DISK        330
 0001F6 47F0 B046           001D8      192           B     AGAIN             CONTINUES UNTIL /* IS REACHED          340
                                       193  *                                                                       350
                                       194  CDEND    CLOSE DSKOUT,CARDF    AN END-OF-FILE IS MARKED ON THE          360
                                       203  *                              DISK BECAUSE OF THE CLOSE                370
                                       204           OPEN  DSKIN                                                    380
                                       212  *                                                                       390
                                       213  MORE     GET   DSKIN                                                    400
 00022A D20A B201 C000 00393 00000     218           MVC   NAME,N                                                   410
 000230 D204 B215 C00B 003A7 0000B     219           MVC   TEMP,T                                                   420
                                       220           PUT   PRINTF                                                   430
                                       225           CNTRL PRINTF,SP,1                                              440
 000250 47F0 B08C           0021E      231           B     MORE           CONTINUES UNTIL END OF FILE               450
                                       232  *                                                                       460
                                       233  DSKEND   CLOSE DSKIN,PRINTF                                             470
                                       242           EOJ                                                            480
                                       245  *                             AREA DESIGNATIONS                         490
 000268                                246  CARDIN   DS    CL80                                                     500
```

```
LOC       OBJECT CODE       ADDR1 ADDR2   STMT   SOURCE STATEMENT                                    FDOS CL3-9 11/01/73

0002B8                                    247           DS    0H                                     505
0002B8                                    248 OUT       DS    CL88   INCLUDES 8 BYTES FOR IOCS       510
                                          249 *                                                      520
000310                                    250           DS    0H                                     521
000310                                    251 IN        DS    CL80                                   522
                                          252 *                                                      560
000360                                    253 PRINT     DS    0CL132                                 570
                                          254 * HEADING.                                             580
000360  4040404040404040                  255           DC    50C' '                                 590
000392  D5C1D4C540D6C640                  256           DC    CL12'NAME OF CITY'                     600
00039E  40404040404040                    257           DC    7C' '                                  610
0003A5  C1E5B40E3C5D4D7                   258           DC    CL9'AV. TEMP.'                         620
0003AE  4040404040404040                  259           DC    54C' '                                 630
                                          260 * SPACES FOR PRINTOUT.                                 640
000360                                    261           ORG   PRINT                                  650
000360                                    262           DS    CL51                                   660
000393                                    263 NAME      DS    CL11                                   670
00039E                                    264           DS    CL9                                    680
0003A7                                    265 TEMP      DS    CL5                                    690
0003AC                                    266           DS    CL56                                   700
                                          267 *                                                      710
000000                                    268 LOGREC    DSECT                                        715
000000                                    269 N         DS    CL11                                   716
00000B                                    270 T         DS    CL5                                    717
000190                                    271           END   START                                  720
0003E8  5B5BC2D6D7C5D540                  272                 =C'$$BOPEN '
0003F0  5B5BC2C3D3D6E2C5                  273                 =C'$$BCLOSE'
0003F8  00000160                          274                 =A(PRINTF)
0003FC  00000000                          275                 =A(CARDF)
000400  00000038                          276                 =A(DSKOUT)
000404  000000D8                          277                 =A(DSKIN)
```

NAME OF CITY	AV. TEMP.
ATLANTA	47.6
BALTIMORE	57.6
BOSTON	51.4
CHICAGO	50.8
COLUMBUS	52.0
DALLAS	65.8
DENVER	49.5
DETROIT	50.1
HARTFORD	49.9
HONOLULU	75.9
LOS ANGELES	64.4
MEMPHIS	61.5
MIAMI	75.1
NEW ORLEANS	69.4
NEW YORK	54.5
PHILA.	53.5
ST. LOUIS	55.3
SALT LAKE	50.9
SAN JUAN	78.3
WASH.,D.C.	57.0

Program Thirteen
Address Modification

The purpose of this program (see statements 1-5) is to store an *array* of card images in core, then print them in a table. Address arithmetic is used for the storage of an array. In doing address arithmetic, the addresses within an instruction are treated as arithmetic numbers.

To illustrate, consider statement 87 which is a variable instruction. The base-displacement addresses are A192 and A0AA. The A192 is the base-displacement address of INFO, the part that has to be changed. According to statement 136, INFO is actually the address of the first byte of the first card image. To get to the second card image, the value of INFO has to be increased by 80. This is done in statements 92 through 94, where the first four bytes of MOVE, namely

D2 4F A1 92

are loaded into a register, then increased by 80, then put back (in statement 94). Remember that registers require fullword data alignment for "move-fullword" instructions. Therefore, statement 86 was provided to make sure that the first byte of MOVE would begin on a fullword boundary. Note that the fifth and sixth bytes of the MVC instruction of MOVE, A0AA, are unaffected.

Another variable instruction is shown in statement 102 where INFO was at the end of the instruction. To make sure that

A1 13 A1 92

would start on a fullword boundary, statement 101 was inserted. This caused the beginning of the MOVOUT instruction, D2, to be in the middle of a fullword, and therefore that the rest of it would be at the proper boundary.

Modification of the variable print instruction (meaning the combination of statements 102 and 103) is accomplished in statements 110 through 113.

In this program, the number of cards was counted in the first part. Then, this number was used in the second part to control the printing. This program is by no means simple. The flowchart and the comments within the program should help to explain the steps.

If there had been a great deal of data, say several hundred or thousands of cards, a problem would have arisen because the displacement within an instruction can be only 12 bits. In other words, the largest displacement from the number in a base register is FFF_x or 4095. In this program, there was no such problem but the method for dealing with the problem is shown in statements 53 through 62, which is also a bit tricky.

In statement 53, register 10 is loaded with the address of FIRST for subsequent usage as the first base register. In statement 54, the address of FIRST (already loaded in register 10) is identified with register 10 as the first base register and the Assembler is also informed that a second base register, namely register 11, can be used when register 10 is "used up." In statement 62, ADCON is defined as the address obtained when 4096 is added to the address of FIRST. In statement 59, this address is placed in register 11 to be used as a base *if necessary*. Statement 61 was needed for execution to branch around the DC.

The unusual order of instructions is due to the fact that ADCON must be addressable (via base register 10) before it is referenced for loading base register 11.

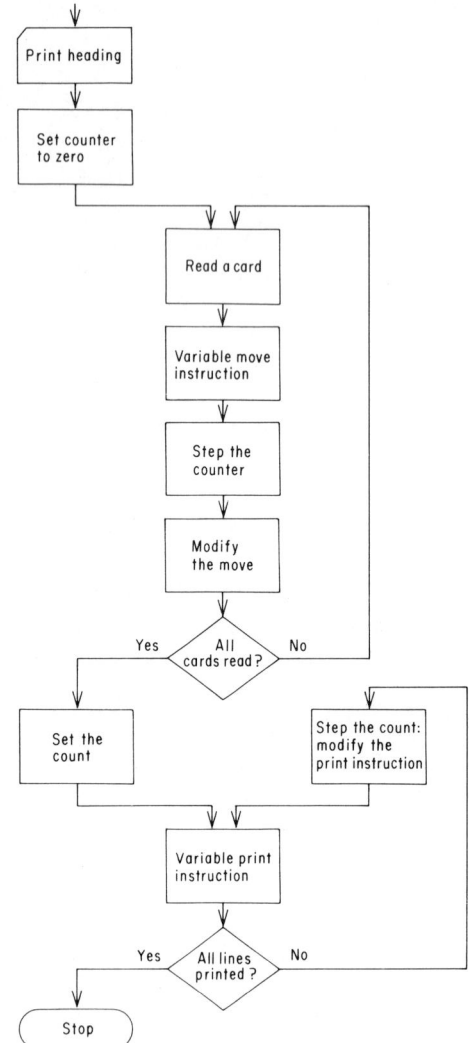

```
// JOB THRTEEN                              10.17.28
* ADDRESS MODIFICATION                                    020
// OPTION LINK
// EXEC ASSEMBLY                                          030


   LOC    OBJECT CODE   ADDR1 ADDR2  STMT  SOURCE STATEMENT                                     FDOS CL3-9 05/29/74

                                       1  * THE PURPOSE OF THIS PROGRAM IS TO STORE AN ARRAY IN CORE. UP TO 50     040
                                       2  * CARDS ARE READ, EACH ONE WITH NAME IN CC 1-30, CODE NUMBER IN CC 31-   050
                                       3  * 34, AND AMOUNT IN CC 61-70.  THE INPUT WAS ON NINE SEPARATE            060
                                       4  * CARDS, AS SHOWN AT THE END.  THIS IS A SIMPLIFIED PROGRAM              061
                                       5  * WITH NO EDITING, JUST FOR DEMONSTRATION.                               062
                                       6              PRINT NOGEN                                                  070
 000100                                7  THRTEEN     START 256      {NOTE THAT $256_{10} = 100_x$}                085
                                       8  * BECAUSE OF THE PRECEDING CARD, THE LOCATIONS ARE ALTERED.              085
                                       9  *                                  DTF SECTION                           090
                                      10  CARDF       DTFCD DEVADDR=SYSRDR,IOAREA1=CARDIN,EOFADDR=OUT              100
                                      31  PRINTF      DTFPR BLKSIZE=132,DEVADDR=SYSLST,IOAREA1=PRINT,CONTROL=YES   110
                                      52  *                                  HOUSEKEEPING SECTION                  130
 000168 05A0                          53  BEGIN       BALR 10,0                                                    140
 C0016A                               54              USING FIRST,10,11       TWO REGISTERS ARE NEEDED, ONE FOR THE  150
                                      55  *                                   FIRST PART OF THE PROGRAM AND ONE FOR 151
                                      56  *                                   THE DATA. A REGISTER WILL ACCOMMODATE 152
                                      57  *                                   ADDRESS DISPLACEMENTS UP TO HEX FFF,  153
                                      58  *                                   OR DECIMAL 4095.                     154
 C0016A 5880 A00A         00174       59  FIRST       L     11,ADCON          THE ADDRESS OF THE INITIAL DISPLACE-  160
                                      60  *                                   MENT FOR GPR 11 IS IN ADCON.         161
 C0016E 47F0 A00E         00178       61              B     START             TO BRANCH AROUND THE NEXT DC         162
 C00172 0000
 C00174 0000116A                      62  ADCON       DC    A(FIRST+4096)                                          163
                                      63  START       OPEN  CARDF,PRINTF                                           170
                                      72              CNTRL PRINTF,SK,1       SKIP TO TOP OF PAGE                  180
 000198 D783 A106 A106 00270 00270    78              XC    PRINT,PRINT                                            190
                                      79  *                                   PROCEDURE SECTION                    200
 00019E F811 A18A A18E 002F4 002F8    80              ZAP   N,ZERO            SET COUNTER TO ZERO                  210
                                      81  AGAIN       GET   CARDF             CARD IMAGE IN CARDIN                 220
 0001B0                               86              CNOP  0,4               FILL TO BEGINNING OF A FULLWORD      230
 0001B0 D24F A1A2 A0B6 0030C 00220    87  MOVE        MVC   INFO,CARDIN                                            240
 0001B6 FA10 A18A B16E 002F4 012D8    88              AP    N,=P'1'           STEPS COUNTER BY 1                   250
                                      89  * THE FOLLOWING THREE INSTRUCTIONS MODIFY THE MOVE INSTRUCTION. THIS     260
                                      90  * TECHNIQUE IS CALLED ADDRESS ARITHMETIC. THE MVC INSTRUCTION HAS SIX    270
                                      91  * BYTES WITH THE INFO ADDRESS AT THE END OF THE FIRST FOUR BYTES.        280
 0001BC 5830 A046         001B0       92              L     3,MOVE            PLACES FIRST FOUR BYTES IN GPR 3     290
 0001C0 5A30 A19E         00308       93              A     3,EIGHTY                                               300
                                      94  * THE DUMP IN THE NEXT INSTRUCTION SHOWS WHAT HAPPENED TO THE MOVE       301
                                      95  * INSTRUCTION IN REGISTER 3 WHEN 80 (BASE 10) OR 50 (HEX) IS ADDED.      302
                                      96  * NOTE THAT THE BASE-DISPLACEMENT ADDRESS, A1A2, BECOMES A1F2, A242      303
                                      97  * A292, AND SO ON AS A RESULT OF THE ADDITION.                           304
                                      98              PDUMP MOVE,MOVE   THIS SHOWS THE CONTENTS OF THE REGISTERS.  305
 0001CE 5030 A046         001B0      103              ST    3,MOVE            REPLACES MODIFIED INSTRUCTION        310
                                     104  *                                                                        320
 0001D2 47F0 A03A         001A4      105              B     AGAIN             REPEATS UNTIL /* IS REACHED          330
                                     106  * A LOOP TO DISPLAY THE ARRAY (UNEDITED). N IS CONVERTED TO BINARY AND   340
                                     107  * GPR 4 IS USED AS A COUNTER.                                            350
 0001D6 F871 A196 A18A 00300 002F4   108  OUT         ZAP   DOUBLE,N                                               360
 0001DC 4F40 A196         00300      109              CVB   4,DOUBLE                                               370
 0001E0 0700                         110              CNOP  2,4               FILL                                 380
 0001E2 D24F A11F A1A2 00289 0030C   111  MOVOUT      MVC   PRINT+25(80),INFO                                      390
```

(Handwritten annotations: "This is 'MOVE'" pointing to line 87; "NOTE THAT $256_{10} = 100_x$" near line 7; "THIS SHOWS THE CONTENTS OF THE REGISTERS." added to line 98)

```
                                                                                                   PAGE    2

        LOC    OBJECT CODE    ADDR1  ADDR2  STMT    SOURCE STATEMENT                    FDOS CL3-9  05/29/74

      C001F4  4640 A092        001FC   112         PUT      PRINTF           PRINTS A CARD IMAGE              400
      C001F8  47F0 A0A2        0020C   117         BCT      4,OVER           IF GPR4 DOES NOT HAVE A 0, BRANCHES  410
      C001FC  5830 A07A        001E4   118         B        CDEND                                             420
      C00200  5A30 A19E        00308   119 OVER    L        3,MOVOUT+2       PLACES END OF MOVOUT IN GPR 3    430
      C00204  5030 A07A        001E4   120         A        3,EIGHTY                                          440
      C00208  47F0 A078        001E2   121         ST       3,MOVOUT+2                                        450
                                       122         B        MOVOUT                                            460
                                       123 *                                                                  470
                                       124 CDEND   CLOSE    CARDF,PRINTF                                      480
                                       133         EOJ                                                        490
                                       136 *                                AREA DESIGNATIONS                 500
      000220                           137 CARDIN  DS       CL80                                              510
      C00270                           138 PRINT   DS       CL132                                             520
      0002F4                           139         DS       0F                                                521
      0002F4                           140 N       DS       PL2              COUNTER                          540
      0002F6  4040                     141         DC       2C' '                                             541
      C002F8  000C                     142 ZERO    DC       PL2'0'                                            550
      C00300                           143 DOUBLE  DS       D                                                 570
      C00308  00000050                 144 EIGHTY  DC       F'80'                                             575
      00030C                           145 INFO    DS       50CL80           FOR 50 CARD IMAGES               530
      000168                           146         END      BEGIN                                             580
      0012B0  5B5BC2D6D7C5D540         147                  =C'$$BOPEN '
      0012B8  5B5BC2D7C4E4D4D7         148                  =CL8'$$BPDUMP'
      0012C0  000001B0000001B0         149                  =A(MOVE,MOVE)
      0012C8  5B5BC2C3D3D6E2C5         150                  =C'$$BCLOSE'
      0012D0  00C00138                 151                  =A(PRINTF)
      0012D4  00000100                 152                  =A(CARDF)
      0012D8  1C                       153                  =P'1'
```

                THRTEEN   05/29/74   *THIS IS REGISTER 3. HERE ARE
                                                THE FIRST TWO HALFWORDS
                                                OF "MOVE" AFTER ONE ADDRESS CHANGE.*   PAGE 1

      GR 0-7   0C0039C0 000039B8 0000FFFF [D24FA1F2] 0000FF84 FFFFFF7C 00000000 000027B8 } DUMP 1
      GR 8-F   0C00430A 0A0107F1 4000286A 0000386A   000037D8 000C47D8 800028B0 000039E0
      FP REG   433E8000 00000000 433E8000 00000000   00000000 00000000 00000000 00000000

                THRTEEN   05/29/74   PAGE 1

      GR 0-7   000039C0 000039B8 0000FFFF D24FA242   0000FF84 FFFFFF7C 00000000 000027B8 } DUMP 2
      GR 8-F   0000430A 0A0107F1 4000286A 0000386A   000037D8 000047D8 900028B0 000039E0
      FP REG   433E8000 00000000 433E8000 00000000   00000000 00000000 00000000 00000000

```
       THRTEEN        05/29/74                                                                    PAGE   1
GR 0-7  0C0039C0 000039B8 0000FFFF D24FA292  0000FF84 FFFFFF7C 00000000 000027B8 ⎫
GR 8-F  0C00430A 0A0107F1 4000286A 0000386A  000037D8 000047D8 900028B0 000039E0 ⎬ DUMP 3
FP REG  433E8000 00000000 433E8000 00000000  00000000 000C0000 00000000 0CC00000 ⎭
```

Note that the displacement has increased by 50_x in each dump.

```
       THRTEEN        05/29/74                                                                    PAGE   1
GR 0-7  0C0039C0 000039B8 0000FFFF D24FA472  0000FF84 FFFFFF7C 00000000 000027B8 ⎫
GR 8-F  0C00430A 0A0107F1 4000286A 0000386A  000037D8 000047D8 900028B0 000039E0 ⎬ LAST DUMP. THE FINAL BASE-DISPLACEMENT IS A472.
FP REG  433E8000 00000000 433E8000 00000000  00000000 00000000 00000000 00000000 ⎭
```

THIS IS THE RESULT (UNEDITED)

                                                                                 CARD NUMBER

```
       SMOOT,ALEX              FB47                .00     620
       HENDERSON,FRANK         3S75            5862.92     630
       HENDERSON,FRANK B       3S23            2379.46     640
       BAND,ALEXANDER          7P18             -37.44     650
       COMENIUS,ALBERT         AB23            8139.58     660
       SMITH,JOHN              FF23               6.23     670
       SMYTH,SAMUEL            FA23              78.99     680
       SMITHSON,HENRY          EB25              39.17     690
       SMYTHE,GEORGE           1323                .23     700
```

The next program makes use of this method of placing an array in core.

Program Fourteen

Program to Demonstrate Internal Sorting and Address Modification

This program uses logical and arithmetic *compare* instructions to interchange sort a set of names. The input cards were as follows:

Von Braun	card 1020	Degaulle	card 1080
Kennedy	card 1030	Lauder	card 1090
Rainier	card 1040	,$ZXPT3	card 1100
Abbazio	card 1050	Yodeler	card 1110
Beatle	card 1060	Burton	card 1120
Dhu	card 1070	,/ZXPT3	card 1130

The problem was to put them into alphabetical order. Where the names are not alphabetical, the IBM code uses a *collating sequence* for characters which depends upon the EBCDIC equivalents. When the green card is used, the following hex equivalents are seen:

$	5B
/	61
,	6B
A	C1
B	C2

and so on, so that there is a logical sequence.

The method is shown in the accompanying flowchart.

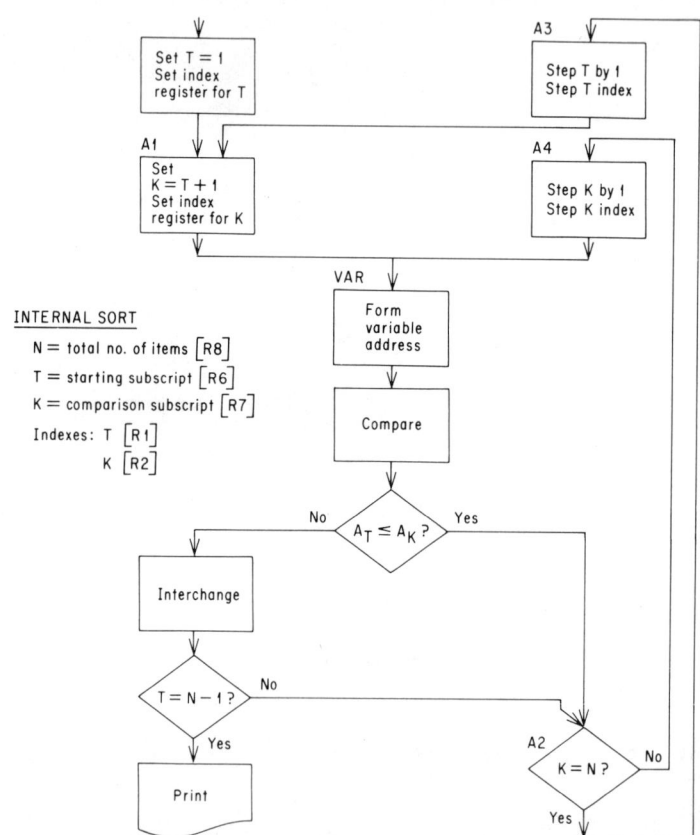

```
// JOB FRTEEN                                                   17.34.02
* PROGRAM TO DEMONSTRATE INTERNAL SORTING AND ADDRESS MODIFICATION    010
// OPTION LINK                                                        020
// EXEC ASSEMBLY                                                      030
```

PAGE   1

```
LOC     OBJECT CODE     ADDR1 ADDR2  STMT   SOURCE STATEMENT                          FDOS CL3-9 11/01/73

                                       1 * IN THIS PROGRAM, UP TO 50 CARDS ARE READ INTO CONSECUTIVE LOCATIONS    040
                                       2 * IN CORE, THEN SORTED INTERNALLY. THIS IS AN INEFFICIENT METHOD OF      050
                                       3 * SORTING BUT DISPLAYS MULTIPLE ADDRESS MODIFICATION. THE ODD NAMES      060
                                       4 * CHOSEN ARE INTENDED TO DISPLAY THE IBM 360 COLLATING SEQUENCE. TWO     070
                                       5 * REGISTERS WERE NEEDED BECAUSE OF THE LARGE STORAGE REQUIREMENT.        080
                                       6           PRINT NOGEN                                                   090
000000                                 7 FRTEEN    START                                                         100
                                       8 *                                DTF SECTION                            110
                                       9 CARDF     DTFCD DEVADDR=SYSRDR,IOAREA1=CARD,EOFADDR=CDEND                120
                                      30 PRINTF    DTFPR BLKSIZE=132,DEVADDR=SYSLST,IOAREA1=PRINT,CONTROL=YES     130
                                      51 *                               HOUSEKEEPING SECTION                    150
000068 05A0                           52 BEGIN     BALR  10,0                                                    160
00006A                                53           USING FIRST,10,11                                             170
00006A 58B0 A00A           00074      54 FIRST     L     11,ADCON                                                180
00006E 47F0 A00E           00078      55           B     START                                                   190
000072 0000
000074 0000106A                       56 ADCON     DC    A(FIRST+4096)                                           200
                                      57 START     OPEN  CARDF,PRINTF                                            210
                                      66           CNTRL PRINTF,SK,1           SKIP TO TOP OF PAGE               220
                                      72           CNTRL PRINTF,SP,3           THREE EXTRA SPACES                230
0000A6 D783 A152 A152 001BC 001BC     78           XC    PRINT,PRINT                                             240
                                      79 *                               PROCEDURE SECTION                      250
                                      80 * PART 1. READ N CARDS INTO CORE.                                       260
0000AC 1B88                           81           SR    8,8                   SET COUNTER TO ZERO               270
                                      82 OVER      GET   CARDF                 CARD IMAGE IN 'CARD'              280
0000BA 0700                           87           CNOP  0,4                   FILL                              290
0000BC D24F A1D6 A102 00240 0016C     88 MOVE      MVC   INFO,CARD                                               300
0000C2 4A80 B1E6           01250      89           AH    8,=H'1'               STEP COUNTER                      310
0000C6 5850 A052           000BC      90           L     5,MOVE                4 BYTES IN GPR 5                  320
0000CA 4A50 B1E8           01252      91           AH    5,=H'80'              MODIFY MOVE INSTRUCTION           330
0000CE 5050 A052           000BC      92           ST    5,MOVE                REPLACE                           340
0000D2 47F0 A044           000AE      93           B     OVER                  REPEATS UNTIL /* IS REACHED       350
                                      94 * PART 2. ALPHABETIZE. THE NAMES ARE IN CC 1-30. REGISTERS ARE RESERVED 360
                                      95 * AS FOLLOWS.                GPR 6 = STARTING SUBSCRIPT, T              370
                                      96 *                            GPR 7 = COMPARISON SUBSCRIPT, K            380
                                      97 *                            GPR 8 = N, THE CARD COUNT                  390
                                      98 *                            GPR 1 = INDEX REGISTER FOR T               400
                                      99 *                            GPR 2 = INDEX REGISTER FOR K               410
0000D6 4860 B1E6           01250     100 CDEND     LH    6,=H'1'               SET T=1                           420
0000DA 4110 A1D6           00240     101           LA    1,INFO                SETS INDEX FOR T                  430
                                     102 * THE FOLLOWING TWO INSTRUCTIONS SET K=T+1                              440
0000DE 1876                          103 A1        LR    7,6                   K=T                               450
0000E0 4A70 B1E6           01250     104           AH    7,=H'1'               K=T+1                             460
                                     105 * THE FOLLOWING THREE INSTRUCTIONS SET THE INDEX REGISTER FOR K IN EACH 470
                                     106 * CASE. WE WANT THE COMPARISON ADDRESS TO BE INFO+80(K-1) WHICH IS THE  480
```

```
LOC       OBJECT CODE      ADDR1  ADDR2   STMT   SOURCE STATEMENT                                    FDOS CL3-9 11/01/73

                                          107 * SAME AS (INFO-80)+80*K                                                490
0000E4  1847                              108          LR      4,7                 K IN GPR4                          500
0000E6  4C40 B1E8               01252     109          MH      4,=H'80'            80K IN GPR4                        510
0000EA  4124 A186               001F0     110          LA      2,INFO-80(4)        INFO-80+80*K                       520
                                          111 * 0(1) IS THE VARIABLE ADDRESS OF THE STARTING FIELD AND 0(2) IS THE    530
                                          112 * ADDRESS OF THE COMPARISON FIELD. BOTH ARE ABSOLUTE.                   540
0000EE  D51D 1000 2000 00000 00000        113 VAR      CLC     0(30,1),0(2)        COMPARES 30 CHARACTERS             550
0000F4  47D0 A0AC               00116     114          BNH     A2                                                     560
                                          115 * THE NEXT THREE INSTRUCTIONS EFFECT THE INTERCHANGE WHERE NECESSARY.   570
0000F8  D24F B176 1000 011E0 00000        116          MVC     STORE,0(1)                                             580
0000FE  D24F 1000 2000 00000 00000        117          MVC     0(80,1),0(2)                                           590
000104  D24F 2000 B176 00000 011E0        118          MVC     0(80,2),STORE                                          600
                                          119 *                                                                       610
00010A  1898                              120          LR      9,8                 N IN GPR9                          620
00010C  4B90 B1E6               01250     121          SH      9,=H'1'             N-1 IN GPR9                        621
000110  1996                              122          CR      9,6                 COMPARE T AND N-1                  630
000112  4780 A0CA               00134     123          BE      PRTOUT              IF EQUAL, BRANCH TO PART 3         640
                                          124 *                                                                       650
000116  1987                              125 A2       CR      8,7                 COMPARE K AND N                    660
000118  4780 A0BE               00128     126          BE      A3                  IF EQUAL, BRANCH TO A3             670
00011C  4A70 B1E6               01250     127 A4       AH      7,=H'1'             STEP K BY 1                        680
000120  4A20 B1E8               01252     128          AH      2,=H'80'            STEP INDEX(K)                      690
000124  47F0 A084               000EE     129          B       VAR                                                    700
000128  4A60 B1E6               01250     130 A3       AH      6,=H'1'             STEP T BY 1                        710
00012C  4A10 B1E8               01252     131          AH      1,=H'80'            STEP INDEX(T)                      720
000130  47F0 A074               000DE     132          B       A1                                                     730
                                          133 * PART 3. THE CARD IMAGES ARE ALPHABETIZED AND READY TO BE LISTED.      740
000134  4190 A186               001F0     134 PRTOUT   LA      9,INFO-80           STARTING ADDRESS MINUS 80 IN R9    750
000138  1878                              135          LR      7,8                 N IN GPR 7, NEEDED FOR BXLE        760
00013A  9856 B1C6               01230     136          LM      5,6,SET             PLACES 1,1 IN GPR 5 AND 6          770
00013E  4A90 B1E8               01252     137 AGAIN    AH      9,=H'80'            SETS INFO IN GPR 9                 780
000142  D24F A16B 9000 001D5 00000        138          MVC     IMAGE,0(9)                                             790
                                          139          PUT     PRINTF              PRINTS ONE LINE                    800
000154  8756 A0D4               0013E     144          BXLE    5,6,AGAIN           THE INDEX IN GPR5 STARTS AT 1,     810
                                          145 *                                    THE INCREMENT IN GPR6 IS           820
                                          146 *                                    ALSO 1 AND THE TERMINAL            830
                                          147 *                                    VALUE IS N IN GPR7                 840
                                          148          CLOSE   CARDF,PRINTF                                           850
                                          157          EOJ                                                            860
                                          160 *                                        AREA DESIGNATIONS              870
00016C                                    161 CARD     DS      CL80                                                   880
0001BC                                    162 PRINT    DS      0CL132                                                 890
0001BC                                    163          DS      CL25                                                   891
0001D5                                    164 IMAGE    DS      CL80                                                   892
000225                                    165          DS      CL27                                                   893
```

```
LOC    OBJECT CODE      ADDR1 ADDR2   STMT   SOURCE STATEMENT                    FDOS CL3-9 11/01/73
000240                                 166 INFO   DS    50CL80                              940
0011E0                                 167 STORE  DS    CL80                                950
001230 00000001                        168 SET    DC    F'1'                                960
001234 00000001                        169        DC    F'1'                                970
000068                                 170        END   BEGIN                               980
001238 5B5BC2D6D7C5D540                171              =C'$$BOPEN '
001240 5B5BC2C3D3D6E2C5                172              =C'$$BCLOSE'
001248 00000038                        173              =A(PRINTF)
00124C 00000000                        174              =A(CARDF)
001250 0001                            175              =H'1'
001252 0050                            176              =H'80'
```

```
,$ZXPT3                MARS            1100
,/ZXPT3                MOON            1130
ABBAZIO,PAOLO          ITALY           1050
BEATLE,WATER           ENGLAND         1060
BURTON,RICHARD         WALES           1120
DEGAULLE,JEAN          FRANCE          1080
DHU,SEAN               IRELAND         1070
KENNEDY,EDWARD         USA             1030
LAUDER,HARRY           SCOTLAND        1090
RAINIER,SAM            MONACO          1040
VON BRAUN,ERIC         GERMANY         1020
YODELER,HANS           SWITZERLAND     1110
```

Appendix for Instructions

The interpretive program supplied by IBM to translate the user's instructions from Assembly language to machine language is called the *Assembler*. The process takes place in two parts (passes). In the first pass, locations are determined for the instructions and data. In the second pass, those instructions which will be present at execution time are translated into machine language.

There are three classes of instructions: (1) those which need to be used during the first pass, but are not translated into machine language; (2) those which are translated on a one-to-one basis from the user's language to machine language; these will be called *simple instructions*; and (3) those which are translated on a one-to-many basis from one line of Assembly language to many lines of machine language; these are called *macro-instructions*.

Some of the instructions which are used during the first pass, but are not translated into machine language, are:

END	To signify the end of a set of program cards, and to tell where the execution of the program is to begin.
PRINT NOGEN	"If additional instructions are generated by the Assembler, don't print them."
START	To set the location counter to the number beginning at card column 15; or if there is no number there, to set the location counter to 0; the number must be on a double-word boundary (divisible by 8).
USING	To inform the Assembler, during the first pass, that the address in the first operand will be placed in the register named in the second operand; if the first operand is an asterisk, the address is the address of the first machine language instruction following the USING.

Some of the macro-instructions which are expanded (translated) into a set of several instructions by the Assembler are:

CNTRL	Which allows the user to control input and output devices, e.g., line-skipping on the printer.
CNOP	Which allows the user to change the position of an instruction; for example:

        CNOP   2,4

means, "If the next instruction does not begin on the second byte of a fullword, put it there." The non-used spaces are filled with NOP ("no operation") instructions.

DTF	Which defines the file.
GET	Which inputs one record.
PUT	Which outputs one record.
CLOSE	To close a file, or more than one file.
EOJ	"End of Job."
OPEN	To open a file, or more than one file.

In the following, a selected set of 99 "simple" instructions is described. They are divided into fourteen categories, as follows:
1. Loading binary numbers
2. Storing binary numbers
3. Binary arithmetic instructions
4. Arithmetic shifts
5. "MOVE" instructions
6. Instructions to change the form of a number
7. Decimal arithmetic instructions
8. "COMPARE" instructions
9. "BRANCH" instructions
10. Special "BRANCH" instructions
11. Logical arithmetic instructions
12. Logical shift instructions
13. Other logical instructions
14. Editing instructions

These instructions are numbered. To find an instruction, use the table which follows. The abbreviations within the descriptions are as follows:

R5 means "register 5"
[R5] means "the contents of R5"
[R5+2] means "the contents of R5, plus 2"
c means that a condition code is set.

In the descriptions, six kinds of instructions are designated, as follows:

RR A two-byte instruction in which both operands are register numbers.

RX A four-byte instruction in which the first operand is a register number and the second operand is the address of an area in core. If the second operand has a number in parenthesis after it, the number is that of an index register.

RS This is a four-byte instruction. There are three types. One type is like LM, where the first two operands are the numbers of registers, and the third operand is the address of a fullword area in core. A second type is the *shift* instruction, where the first operand is the number of a register and the second operand is the number of bits to be shifted.

SI A four-byte instruction in which the first operand is the address of one byte in core, and the second operand is an actual datum, e.g., X'3', or C'$'.

SS1 A six-byte instruction in which both operands are addresses of areas in core, the length of *both* operands being given by the length of the *first* operand.

SS2 Like SS1 except that each operand has its own length.

In the case of SS1 or SS2, the length may be given by a number in parentheses directly following the name of the area. If it is not, the Assembler inserts the length according to that in the Area Designations within the program.

Appendix for Instructions

Table: The 99 Selected Fixed-Point Instructions*

A	15	BNM	62	DP	40	MVN	32	SLL	82
AH	16	BNO	63	DR	19	MVO	33	SLR	80
AL	77	BNP	64	ED	98	MVZ	34	SP	42
ALR	78	BNZ	65	EDMK	99	N	85	SR	25
AP	39	BP	66	IC	1	NC	86	SRA	28
AR	17	BR	67	L	2	NI	87	SRDA	29
B	52	BXH	75	LA	3	NOP	69	SRDL	83
BAL	71	BXLE	76	LCR	4	NOPR	70	SRL	84
BALR	72	BZ	68	LH	5	NR	88	ST	11
BC	53	C	44	LM	6	O	89	STC	12
BCR	54	CH	45	LNR	7	OC	90	STH	13
BCT	73	CL	46	LPR	8	OI	91	STM	14
BCTR	74	CLC	47	LR	9	OR	92	TM	97
BE	55	CLI	48	LTR	10	PACK	37	UNPK	38
BH	56	CLR	49	M	20	S	23	X	93
BL	57	CP	50	MH	21	SH	24	XC	94
BM	58	CR	51	MP	41	SL	79	XI	95
BNE	59	CVB	36	MR	22	SLA	26	XR	96
BNH	60	CVD	36	MVC	30	SLDA	27	ZAP	43
BNL	61	D	18	MVI	31	SLDL	81		

*The numbers next to the instructions tell where the description of the instruction can be found in the following listing. For example, LTR is the tenth instruction described below.

GROUP I. LOADING BINARY NUMBERS

1. IC: Insert Character. (RX)

IC	2,ALPHA	Takes the first byte of ALPHA and copies it into the low-order (rightmost) position in R2.
IC	6,=X'A7'	Copies 10100111 into the low-order byte of R6.

2. L: Load. (RX)

L	7,ALPHA	Copies fullword ALPHA into R7.
L	1,A(4)	[R4] + A is calculated and the fullword at that address is copied into R1.

3. LA: Load Address. (RX)

LA	3,ALPHA	Copies fullword address of ALPHA into R3.
LA	7,10(3)	[R3 + 10] is calculated and copied into R7.
LA	7,10(3,5)	[R3] + [R5] + 10 is calculated and copied into R7.
LA	3,B(0)	When R0 is used as an index register, its contents are considered to be 0, even if it is not. This is the same in effect as LA 3,B.

4. LCR: Load Complement. (RR,c)

LCR	7,8	Copies contents of R8, with sign changed, into R7.
LCR	4,4	Changes the sign of the contents of R4.

5. LH: Load Halfword. (RX)

LH	6,GAMMA	GAMMA, defined as a halfword, is copied into the low-order half of R6, and the high-order bit of GAMMA is propagated all the way to the left in R6.
LH	7,=H'24'	Calculates the binary equivalent of decimal 24, and

6. LM: Load Multiple (RS)

LM   1,3,N

LM   14,2,M

LM   12,10,SAVE

LM   2,4,700(8)

7. LNR: Load Negative (RR,c)

LNR   3,2

LNR   3,3

copies the result into R7, propagating the high-order bit to the left.

Loads three consecutive fullwords, beginning with the one at N, into registers 1,2,3.
Loads five consecutive fullwords, beginning with the one at M, into registers 14,15,0,1,2; this is called *wraparound*.
Loads 15 consecutive fullwords, beginning with the one at SAVE, into registers 12,13,14,15,0,1,2,3,4,5,6,7,8,9,10; this is useful if, for example, R11 is the *base register* and all the other registers are needed temporarily; then the contents of the registers are stored in SAVE by an STM instruction and brought back by this LM instruction.
Calculates [R8 + 700], then loads three consecutive fullwords beginning at that address into registers 2,3,4.

If [R2] are negative, they are copied into R3; otherwise, the sign is changed to negative (by complementing) and the result is copied into R3.
See above.

8. LPR: Load Positive (RR,c)

LPR   3,2

LPR   3,3

9. LR: Load Register (RR)

LR   12,5

10. LTR: Load and Test (RR,c)

LTR   1,2

LTR   13,13

If [R2] are positive, they are copied into R3; otherwise the sign is changed to positive (by complementing) and the result is copied into R3.
See above; this results in the absolute value.

Copies [R5] into R12.

Copies [R2] into R1 and sets a condition code.
Sets the condition code; useful if the programmer wishes to find out whether a binary fullword is positive, zero, or negative.

GROUP II. STORING BINARY NUMBERS

11. ST: Store (RX)

ST   7,A

ST   6,B(7)

12. STC: Store Character (RX)

STC   2,A(5)

STC   4,B+2(15)

Copies [R7] into A, which must be defined as a fullword.
Calculates [R7] + B; [R6] is copied into that address which must be on a fullword boundary.

Calculates [R5] + A; copies the low-order byte of R2 into that location.
Calculates [R15] + B + 2; copies the low-order byte of R4 into that location.

Appendix for Instructions

13. STH: Store Halfword (RX)

STH	10,C	Copies the low-order halfword of R10 into C, which must be on a halfword boundary.
STH	10,C(4)	Calculates [R4] + C, which must be on a halfword boundary, then copies the low-order halfword of R10 into that location.

14. STM: Store Multiple (RS)

STM	1,5,A	Copies the contents of registers 1 through 5 into five consecutive fullwords beginning with A.
STM	4,2,A	Copies the contents of registers 4,5,6,7,8,9,10,11,12,13,14,15,0,1,2 into the fifteen consecutive fullword areas beginning with A.
STM	2,4,700(6)	Calculates [R6] + 700 which must be on a fullword boundary, then copies the contents of registers 2,3,4 into the three consecutive fullword areas beginning at that address.

GROUP III. BINARY ARITHMETIC INSTRUCTIONS

15. A: Add (RX,c)

A	5,N	Adds the fullword at N to [R5], leaving the sum in R5.
A	2,P(7)	Calculates [R7] + the fullword at P, then adds the fullword at that address to [R2], leaving the result in R2.

16. AH: Add Halfword (RX,c)

AH	1,=H'4'	Converts decimal 4 to binary and adds the result into R1.
AH	3,C	Adds the halfword at C into R3.
AH	15,X(3)	Calculates the sum of [R3] and X, which must be on a halfword boundary, then adds the halfword there into R15.

17. AR: Add Registers (RR,c)

AR	12,4	[R4] is added to [R12], with the sum left in R12.

18. D: Divide (RX)

Let the dividend (numerator) be NUM and the divisor (denominator) be a fullword DEN. If NUM is a doubleword, proceed as follows:

LM	2,3,NUM	Loads NUM in R2 and R3.
D	2,DEN	The quotient forms in R3 and the remainder in R2.
ST	3,QUOT	The quotient is stored in QUOT.

If NUM is a fullword, proceed as follows:

L	2,NUM	Loads NUM into R2.
SRDA	2,32	Shifts NUM right 32 bits, to R3, propagating the sign throughout R2.
D	2,DEN	As above.
ST	3,QUOT	As above.

In both cases, the work is done with an "even-odd" *pair* of registers, of which the first one is always even-numbered.

19. DR: Divide Registers (RR)

Using the abbreviations of 18, with NUM and DEN defined as fullwords, proceed as follows:

Assembly Language Basics

L	6,NUM	Load into even-numbered register.
SRDA	6,32	Shift right 32 bits into R7; the sign bit is propagated at the left throughout R6.
L	11,DEN	Load into any other available register.
DR	6,11	Quotient forms in R7, remainder in R6.
ST	6,QUOT	Quotient stored in QUOT.

20. M: Multiply (RX)

For fullwords, the procedure is as follows:

L	3,RATE	Multiplicand into any odd register.
M	2,TIME	Multiplier into even register; the product forms in the paired registers R2 and R3.
STM	2,3DIST	The doubleword answer is stored in doubleword DIST.

21. MH: Multiply Halfword (RX)

For halfwords, the procedure is as follows:

LH	6,MASS	Multiplicand into any register.
MH	6,VELOC	Result spreads in R6 alone. Instead of this, one can use a self-defining operand, for example: MH 6,=H'25'.
ST	6,MOMENT	The fullword answer is stored in fullword MOMENT.

22. MR: Multiply Registers (RR)

For fullwords, the procedure is as follows:

L	5,FORCE	Any register can be used.
L	3,DIST	Must be an odd register.
MR	2,5	The product forms in R2,R3 (paired).
STM	2,3,WORK	The product is stored in a doubleword.

Note particularly the method for squaring a number:

L	5,=F'6'	Loads the fullword binary equivalent of decimal 6 into R5.
MR	4,5	Forms the binary equivalent of decimal 36 in registers 4 and 5.

The first operand of the MR instruction must be an even-numbered register, but the number is loaded into the odd (rightmost) half of the pair.

23. S: Subtract (RX,c)

S	12,N	Subtracts the fullword at N from [R12], leaving the difference as the contents of R12.
S	4,M(5)	Calculates the address by adding M and the contents of R5, then subtracts the value of this from [R4], result in R4.

24. SH: Subtract Halfword (RX,c)

SH	1,=H'5'	Subtracts a binary halfword, equivalent to decimal 5, from [R1], result in R1.
SH	3,A(7)	Calculates the address by adding A to [R7], which must be on a halfword boundary, then subtracts this from the value at [R3], result in R3.

25. SR: Subtract Registers (RR,c)

SR	1,3	Subtracts [R3] from [R1], result in R1.
SR	5,5	Sets R5 to zero.

Appendix for Instructions

GROUP IV. ARITHMETIC SHIFTS

26. SLA: Shift Left Algebraic (RS,c)

SLA   9,3 — Shifts the 32 bits of R9 three bits to the left, except for the sign bit which is left unchanged. (Three zero bits are filled in at the right.) The arithmetic result is multiplication by 2 * 2 * 2 = 8. If a bit unlike the sign bit is shifted out, an error condition [overflow] is reported; zeros are padded at the right.

SLA   9,0(5) — The amount of shift is in R5.

27. SLDA: Shift Left Double Algebraic (RS,c)

SLDA   4,26 — As in instruction 26, except that R4 and R5 are paired (linked); the sign bit is the high-order bit of R4; as with all instructions which link registers, the instruction is addressed to the even half of the two registers.

28. SRA: Shift Right Algebraic (RS,c)

SRA   7,3 — Shifts the contents of R7 three bits to the right, filling in with sign bits at the left. Each shift of one bit is a division by 2 with a loss of the remainder, if any; +5 becomes +2 and -5 becomes -3.

29. SRDA: Shift Right Double Algebraic (RS,c)

SRDA   12,5 — As in instruction 28, except that R12 and R13 are linked. The sign bit is the high-order bit of R12.

GROUP V. "MOVE" INSTRUCTIONS

30. MVC: Move in Core (SS1)

For most beginning students, this is the instruction that causes the first serious problems. *The length of the first operand is assumed for both operands.*

MVC   A,B — Assembler looks in the area designations for the length of A. Then, starting at the left of the area described as B, assembler copies as many bytes from B to A, from (B+1) to (A+1), from (B+2) to (A+2), as is given in the length of the first operand, here, A.

MVC   A(5),B — Copies 5 characters (bytes) starting at B into A, from (B+1) into (A+1), up to (B+4) into (A+4), a total of exactly 5 characters; the length given in parentheses for the first operand *overrides* the length of A given in the area designations.

MVC   A+2(5),B — Like the above, except that the byte at B is copied into A+2, and so on, until the byte at B+4 is copied into A+6.

MVC   7(5,11),6(12) — The address of the first operand is [R11 + 7]. The address of the second operand is [R12 + 6]. Five characters are copied, as described above.

Assembly Language Basics

31. MVI: Move Immediate (SI)

MVI	CARD,C' '	A blank (one byte) is copied into the byte at CARD.
MVI	A+2,C'$'	Places a dollar sign at A+2, which is the *third* byte of A.
MVI	0(1),C'-'	Places a minus sign at the address in R1.
MVI	3(4),C'+'	Calculates [R4 + 3], then places a plus sign at that address.

32. MVN: Move Numerics (SS1)

A byte has 8 bits. We shall call the first four bits the *left nibble*, and the second four bits the *right nibble*.

MVN	A+2(1),B+4	Copies the right nibble of B+4 into the right nibble of A+2.
MVN	A+2(3),B+4	Copies the right nibbles of B+4, B+5, and B+6 into the right nibbles of A+2, A+3, and A+4, respectively.
MVN	A,B	The length of A is assumed; that number of right nibbles are copied from B into A.
MVN	FLD+3(2),=X'FA27'	The right nibbles of the sending operand are A and 7; the A is copied into the right nibble of FLD+3, and the 7 is copied into the right nibble of FLD+4.

33. MVO: Move with Offset (SS2)

This is a difficult instruction with *two* lengths either expressed in parentheses or else taken from the area designations. In the following examples, assume FLD has a length of 4 and contains 12 34 56 7S, where S is the nibble giving the *sign* of FLD.

MVO	FLD(4),FLD(3)	Copies the first 3 bytes of FLD into 3½ bytes of FLD, filling at the left with zeros; in this case, FLD becomes 01 23 45 6S; note that the "offset" is one nibble.
MVO	FLD(4),FLD(2)	Copies the first 2 bytes into 3½ bytes, yielding 00 01 23 4S.
MVO	FLD(3),FLD(4)	Avoid.

34. MVZ: Move Zones (SS1)

See instruction 32. The difference is that the *left* nibbles are moved, instead of the right nibbles.

MVC	A(3),B	The left nibble of B is copied into the left nibble of A, then the left nibble of B+1 is copied into the left nibble of A+1, and finally the left nibble of B+2 is copied into the left nibble of A+2.
MVZ	FLD+3(1),=X'F0'	If FLD is F1F2F3D4, the result is F1F2F3F4; it would have been the same if the second operand had been, for example, =X'FB'.

GROUP VI. CHANGING THE FORM OF A NUMBER

35. CVB: Convert to Binary (RX)

CVB	4,A	A must be in core as a packed number in a doubleword area; the result is the binary equivalent fullword in R4; the usual error is forgetting to define A as a doubleword.

36. CVD: Convert to Decimal (Packed) (RX)

CVD	4,A	A must be defined as a doubleword; the fullword in R4 is converted to a packed

Appendix for Instructions

doubleword; estimates may show that the second half of the doubleword contains all of the packed number, with the left fullword all zeros.

37. PACK: (SS2)

The purpose of this instruction is to change a number from *zoned* (or unpacked) form into *packed* form. It is a two-length instruction; ordinarily, the lengths are taken from the area designations. If decimal arithmetic instructions are to be used, the packed form is needed. If binary arithmetic is to be done, the packed word must be converted to binary; in that case, the first operand should be defined as a doubleword.

PACK   A,B   Zoned B is packed into A. In the following, S stands for the sign nibble. If B contains F1F2S3 (which is of the form ZL3), then it can be packed most economically as 12 3S (which is a PL2). If binary arithmetic is to be done, A should be defined as a double word (8 bytes) and the result will be 00 00 00 00 00 00 12 3S.

PACK   A,A   Zoned A is packed into itself with zeros padding the left.

38. UNPK: Unpack (SS2)

The purpose of this instruction is to change a number from *packed* form (which is used for decimal arithmetic) into *zoned* form (which is used for printing the result).

UNPK   C,D   D is a packed number; the unpacked, or zoned, number is formed in C; it is necessary to "scale" the number so that C is long enough to hold the result; for example, the PL4 packed number 12 34 56 7S becomes F1 F2 F3 F4 F5 F6 S7, requiring, in this case, at least 7 bytes, ZL7.

GROUP VII. DECIMAL ARITHMETIC INSTRUCTIONS

39. AP: Add Packed (SS2,c)

For AP and SP (instruction 42), note the following conditions: (1) the first operand must be long enough to contain the result; (2) if there are implied decimal points in the numbers, the numbers must have previously been aligned properly; (3) a number can be added to or subtracted from itself; (4) in the machine language translation of the instruction, each of the four-bit lengths is represented by a number one less than the actual length (often puzzling to students); this was done for the convenience of the hardware designer.

AP   B,A   If B is 12 34 5+ and A is 01 0+ at the beginning, the result (in B) is 12 35 5+; if B is 12 34 5+ and A is 12 34˙5-, then the result (in B) is 00 00 0+; if B is 12 3+ and A is 45 67 8+, then the result is an interrupt and an error message; if B is 12 3+ and A is 00 00 1+, the result (in B) is 12 4+.

40. DP: Divide Packed (SS2)

In this instruction, (1) the divisor (denominator) may not have more than 15 decimal digits; (2) the quotient may not have more than 31 decimal digits; (3) a remainder is formed of precisely the same length as the divisor; (4) the result appears in the order QUOTIENT |REMAINDER which is the reverse of the situation in binary division. In the following example, assume that the area designations are:

NUM	DS	PL4	12 34 5ᴧ6 7S
DEN	DS	PL3	12 3ᴧ4 5S
RESULT	DS	0PL9	
QUOT	DS	PL6	01 23 45 67ᴧ89 0S
REM	DS	PL3	12 34 5S

where the symbol ᴧ indicates an implied decimal point. Then a suggested procedure for dividing is:

```
ZAP     RESULT,NUM        (see instruction 43)
MP      RESULT,=P'1000'   (see instruction 41)
DP      RESULT,DEN
```

The quotient forms in QUOT. If it is known to be positive, it may be half-adjusted as follows:

```
AP      QUOT,=P'5'
MVO     QUOT,QUOT (5)
```

41. MP: Multiply Packed (SS2)

In this instruction, (1) the multiplier must be no more than 15 decimal digits in length, and (2) the product must be no more than 31 digits in length. In the example which follows, assume that the area designations are:

NMBR	DS	PL3	12 3ᴧ4 5S
MPLR	DS	PL2	12ᴧ3S
PROD	DS	PL5	01 23 45ᴧ67 8S

then the following procedure finds the product to the nearest hundredth, assuming the product is positive:

```
ZAP     PROD,NMBR     (see instruction 43)
MP      PROD,MPLR
AP      PROD,=P'5'
MVO     PROD,PROD(4)
```

42. SP: Subtract Packed (SS2,c)

See instruction 39 for the rules. To find A - B, the following procedure is suggested:

```
ZAP     DIFF,A
SP      DIFF,B
```

which now has DIFF = A - B

43. ZAP: Zero and Add Packed (SS2,c)

ZAP   B(3),A(2)   First the three first bytes of B are set to zero, then the first two bytes of A are added (right-adjusted).

GROUP VIII. "COMPARE" INSTRUCTIONS

44. C: Compare (RX,c)

C   12,B   Simulates the subtraction of fullword [B] from [R12]; both operands are left unchanged but a condition code is set telling what the result of the subtraction would have been, i.e., zero, negative, or positive.

45. CH: Compare Halfword (RX,c)

CH   9,LIMIT   Simulates [R9] - [LIMIT] exactly as in instruction 44, except that LIMIT is defined as a halfword.

46. CL: Compare Logical (RX,c)

The logical COMPARE's (instructions 46,47,48,49) are used mainly for alphabetic data, although they may be used for numeric as well. Instead of simulating a subtraction, as in the arithmetic compares (instructions 44,45,50,51), they start at the left ends of the items to be compared and travel left to right stopping if and when there is a difference. If the data are binary, the sign bits are considered as data rather than as signs. If the two items are

Appendix for Instructions

exactly the same, the condition code is set to 0. If, at some point, one item differs from the other, the condition code is set at 1 or 2 depending upon which is "higher." If the data are alphabetic, the EBCDIC representation determines which is the "higher."

    CL   1,A   A must be a fullword; this is compared (left to right) with the fullword in R1.

47. CLC: Compare Logical in Core (SS1,c)
    CLC   P,Q   The length compared is assumed to be that of P. If P is a CL5 'SMITH' and Q is a CL8 'SMITHSON', only the first five bytes will be compared and the condition code will be set to zero; if P is a CL5'SMITH' and Q is a CL6'SMYTHE', only the first five characters will be compared and (because I comes before Y) the condition code will be set to 1.

48. CLI: Compare Logical Immediate (SI,c)
    CLI   P,B'10011110'   The second operand must be one byte; it may be binary (B), hex (X) or a character (C); only one byte at P is compared logically.

49. CLR: Compare Logical Registers (RR,c)
    CLR   8,9   The contents of R8 and R9 are compared from left to right, treating the sign bits as data.

50. CP: Compare Packed (SS2,c)
    CP   A,B   Simulates A - B; see instruction 44; A and B must be packed numbers.

51. CR: Compare Registers (RR,c)
    CR   8,9   Simulates [R8] - [R9], unlike instruction 49; see instruction 44.

GROUP IX. "BRANCH" INSTRUCTIONS

There are seven sets of instructions which set condition codes:
1. Loads: LCR, LNR, LPR, LTR
2. Binary Arithmetic: A,AH,AR,S,SH,SR,AL,ALR,SL,SLR
3. Binary Shifts: SLA,SLDA,SRA,SRDA,SLL,SLDL,SRL,SRDL
4. Decimal Arithmetic: ZAP,AP,SP (but not MP or DP)
5. Compares: C,CH,CR,CP,CLR,CL,CLI,CLC
6. Logic: ANDs, ORs, exclusive ORs
7. TRT, TM, ED, EDMK, and some others.

When the condition code is set to 0,1,2, or 3, it is possible to use a *branch on condition* type of instruction using, instead of the condition code, a *mask bit* within the branch instruction. (This will be demonstrated.) The mask bits are 8,4,2,1 corresponding to the condition codes 0,1,2,3. There are also *unconditional branch* instructions, which will be discussed in this group, and some more complicated, but very useful, branch instructions in Group X.

52. B: Branch Unconditionally (RX)
    B   PART2   At this point, execution of the program to the instruction with the label "PART2".

53. BC: Branch on Condition (RX)
When a condition code is set after an arithmetic

instruction or an algebraic COMPARE, the condition codes and mask bits are usually as follows:

First operand - Second operand C.C. M.B.
   zero   0   8
   negative   1   4
   positive   2   2
   overflow   3   1

The "overflow" condition code occurs with only certain instructions (see green card or manual). For logical operations, the corresponding interpretations are:

   equal   0   8
   first operand low   1   4
   second operand low   2   2

For so-called logical arithmetic (AL and SL), used in double-precision work:

   zero, no carry   0   8
   no zero, no carry   1   4
   zero, carry   2   2
   no zero, carry   3   1

For other instructions, consult the green card or a manual.

BC	8,RT	If the condition code set was 0, branch to the instruction labeled RT; otherwise, go to the NSI (next sequential instruction).
BC	4,RT	If the condition code set was 1, branch to the instruction labeled RT; otherwise, NSI
BC	7,RT	If the condition code set was 1, 2, or 3 corresponding to mask bits of 4, 2, or 1, then branch; otherwise NSI.
BC	11,RT	This corresponds to mask bits of 8, 2, and 1 or condition codes 0, 2, 3.
BC	13,RT	This corresponds to mask bits of 8, 4, or 1 or condition codes of 0, 1, 3.
BC	15,RT	Since 15 = 8 + 4 + 2 + 1, this corresponds to condition codes of 0, 1, 2, or 3, in other words all possibilities. This is, then, an unconditional branch.

In most cases, it is more convenient to use the *extended mnemonic instruction codes* which are shown as instructions 55 to 70.

54. BCR: Branch on condition to an address in a register (RR)

BCR	8,9	If the condition code was 0, corresponding to a mask bit of 8, branch to the address in R9; otherwise, NSI.

55. BE: Branch if Equal (RX)

CP	A,B	Compare A and B.
BE	ROUT1	If A and B are equal, branch to Routine 1, otherwise NSI; this is the same as BC 8,ROUT1.

56. BH: Branch if High (RX)

CP	A,B	Compare A and B.
BH	ROUT1	If A is larger than B, branch to Routine 1, otherwise NSI; this is the same as BC 2,ROUT1.

57. BL: Branch if Low (RX)

CP	A,B	Compare A and B.

Appendix for Instructions

BL	ROUT1	If A is smaller than B, branch to Routine 1, otherwise NSI; this is the same as BC 4,ROUT1.

58. BM: Branch on Minus (RX)

SP	A,B	Find A−B (replaces A).
BM	ROUT1	If the result is negative, branch to Routine 1, otherwise NSI.
AP	A,B	Find A+B (replaces A).
BM	ROUT1	Same as above.

The BM instruction is identical BC 4,ROUT1.

59. BNE: Branch if Not Equal (RX)

CP	A,B	Compare A and B.
BNE	OVER	If they are not equal, branch to OVER, otherwise NSI; this is identical with BC 7,OVER.

60. BNH: Branch if Not High (RX)

CP	A,B	Compare A and B.
BNH	AGAIN	If A is not higher than B, branch to AGAIN, otherwise NSI; this is identical with BC 13,AGAIN.

61. BNL: Branch if Not Low (RX)

CP	A,B	Compare A and B.
BNL	MORE	If A is not lower than B, branch to MORE, otherwise NSI; this is identical to BC 11,MORE.

62. BNM: Branch if Not Minus (RX)

LTR	3,3	
BNM	NM	If the fullword in R3 is not minus, branch to NM, otherwise NSI; this is identical to BC 11,NM.

63. BNO: Branch if Not Ones (RX)

TM	A,X'0E'	Compares the first byte of A with binary 00001110; the second operand is called the *mask*; the one byte at A is compared with the mask, but only where there are ones in the mask; the next instruction now makes the actual decision.
BNO	OUT	If the bits opposite the ones in the mask are not all ones, branch to OUT, otherwise NSI; this is identical to BC 14,OUT.

64. BNP: Branch if Not Positive (RX)

AR	2,3	Adds [R3] into R2.
BNP	RTN7	If the result is not positive, branch to RTN7, otherwise NSI; this is identical with BC 13,RTN7.

65. BNZ: Branch if Not Zero (RX)

SP	A,B	Forms A−B replacing A.
BNZ	P3	If the result is not zero, branch to the instruction labeled P3; this is identical to BC 7,P3.

66. BP: Branch if Positive (RX)

ZAP	A,A	In this case, the result is to set the condition code.
BP	POS	If the result is positive, branch to the instruction labeled POS, otherwise NSI; this is identical to BC 2,POS.

67. BR: Unconditional Branch to Register Address (RR)

BR   7   Unconditional branch to the address in Register 7; this is the same as BCR 15,7.

68. BZ: Branch on Zero (RX)

AH   8,=H'63'   Adds the halfword equivalent of decimal 63 to [R8], result in R8.

BZ   ZERO   If the result is zero, branch to the instruction labeled ZERO, otherwise NSI; this is identical to BC 8,ZERO.

69. NOP: NO Operation (RX)

NOP   OUT   This is the same as BC 0,OUT; its purpose is to fill a space of 4 bytes, sometimes necessary to place the next instruction on a required boundary.

70. NOPR: No Operation (RR)

NOPR   9   This is the same as BCR 0,9; like the preceding except that it fills a space of 2 bytes.

GROUP X. SPECIAL "BRANCH" INSTRUCTIONS

71. BAL: Branch and Link (RX)

BAL   15,SKIP   (1) Loads the address of the NSI (next sequential instruction) in R15, then (2) branches to SKIP.

BAL   4,NEXT(5)   (1) Calculates the sum of [R5] and NEXT, (2) loads the address of the NSI in R4, then (3) branches to the calculated address.

72. BALR: Branch and Link Register (RR)

BALR   15,13   (1) Loads the address of the NSI into R15, then (2) branches to the address in R13.

BALR   12,0   (1) Loads the address of the NSI into R12, then (2) continues to the NSI; the purpose is to get the address of the NSI into a register; in elementary programs, this is commonly paired with a USING.

73. BCT: Branch on Count (RX)

The main purpose of this instruction is to go through a *loop* a specified number of times:

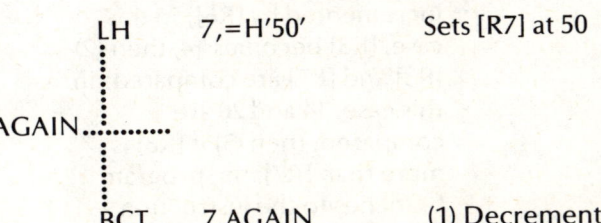

LH   7,=H'50'   Sets [R7] at 50

AGAIN...........

BCT   7,AGAIN   (1) Decrements R7 by 1, (2) if [R7] is not zero, branches back to AGAIN, otherwise continues to the NSI; in this case, it will go through the loop 50 times.

Appendix for Instructions

74. BCTR: Branch on Count to Address in Register (RR)

BCTR   10,12   (1) Decrements R10 by 1, (2) if [R10] is not zero, branches to the address in R12, otherwise goes to the NSI.

BCTR   10,0   (1) Decrements R10 by 1, (2) then continues to the NSI; the same purpose can be served (more slowly) by
SH   10,=H'1'.

75. BXH: Branch on Index High (RS)

This instruction has three operands: the first is the number of a register and is called the *index*; if the second is the number of an *even* register, it is linked with the next register and these two registers are, respectively, the *increment* register and the *limit* register; the third operand is the address (label) of the instruction to which the program will branch. In the following, assume that [R3] = 11, [R6] = 3, and [R7] = 20.

BXH   3,6,LOOP   (1) First, the index [R3] is incremented by [R6]; in this case, [R3] becomes 14, then (2) [R3] and [R7] are compared; in this case, 14 and 20 are compared, then (3) if [R3] is more than [R7], the program branches to the instruction called LOOP, otherwise NSI; in this case, because 14 is not more than 20, the program continues to the NSI; as the program continues to meet this instruction, the index becomes 17, 20, and, finally, 23, at which time it branches to LOOP.

If the second operand is the number of an *odd* register, the contents of that register are treated as being both increment and limit.

76. BXLE: Branch on Index Low or Equal (RS)

Like the preceding, this instruction has three operands with the same properties and names. The difference is that the branch takes place when the index is less than or equal to the limit. In the following, assume that [R3] = 11, [R6] = 3, and [R7] = 20.

BXLE   3,6,LOOP   (1) and (2) are as in instruction 75; then (3) if [R3] is less than or equal to [R7], the program branches to LOOP, otherwise to the NSI; in this case, because 14 is less than 20, the program will branch.

GROUP XI. LOGICAL ARITHMETIC

The main purpose of the logical arithmetic instructions is to do multiple precision addition and subtraction. After a logical arithmetic instruction, one of the following condition codes is set. For convenience, the corresponding mask bits and interpretation are given.

Condition code	Mask bit	Interpretation
0	8	zero, no carry
1	4	no zero, no carry
2	2	zero, carry
3	1	no zero, carry

77. AL: Add Logical (RX,c)
In the following example, A, B, and C are defined as doublewords. It is required to find A + B and store the doubleword result in C. (This simulates a doubleword add instruction.)

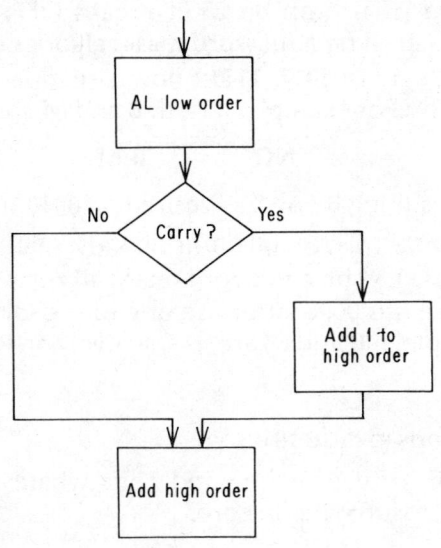

```
       LM    0,1,A
       AL    1,B+4
       BC    12,CONT
       AH    0,=H'1'
CONT   A     0,B
       STM   0,1,C
```

78. ALR: Add Logical Register (RR,c)
ALR   5,6   Adds [R6] to [R5] logically, i.e., disregarding the sign and setting a condition code, with the sum in R5.

79. SL: Subtract Logical (RX,c)
In the following example, the conditions are as in instruction 77 except that it is required to find A - B and store it in C.

```
         LM    3,4,A
         SL    4,B+4
         BC    3,AROUND
         SH    3,=H'1'        or BCTR  3,0
AROUND   S     3,B
         STM   3,4,C
```

80. SLR: Subtract Logical Register (RR,c)
SLR   3,4   Like 78; the difference forms in R3.

GROUP XII. LOGICAL SHIFT INSTRUCTIONS

In the four instructions which follow, all the bits in the registers are considered to be data, i.e., there are no sign bits. The high-order bit in the register, ordinarily regarded as the sign bit, is not treated as such and therefore is not propagated during a shift as in the algebraic shifts. No condition codes are set. The main purpose of these instructions is to isolate parts of a fullword or doubleword. This problem occurs when, for example, a fullword or doubleword is a code describing a customer or a product and a particular part of it is to be separated for the purpose of making a decision.

81. SLDL: Shift Left Double Logical (RS)
SLDL   6,9   The contents of registers 6 and 7 are shifted left 9 bits, padding with zeros at the right; the first operand must be even.

82. SLL: Shift Left Logical (RS)
SLL   3,2   The contents of R3 are shifted

Appendix for Instructions

left 2 bits, padding with zeros to the right.

83. SRDL: Shift Right Double Logical (RS)
SRDL   10,14   The contents of registers 10 and 11 are shifted right 14 bits with padding of zeros to the left; the first operand must be even.

84. SRL: Shift Right Logical (RS)
SRL   5,13   The contents of R5 are shifted right 13 bits with zeros padded at the left.

GROUP XIII. OTHER LOGICAL INSTRUCTIONS

The thirteen logical instructions which follow are used for (a) bit manipulation and (b) bit testing. The first twelve are AND's (N, NC, NI, NR), OR's (O, OC, OI, OR), and Exclusive OR's (X, XC, XI, and XR). The most convenient use for these is to turn bits ON or OFF, or to switch bits. (A bit is considered to be ON if it is a *one* and OFF if it is a *zero*.) These first twelve instructions can also be used to test for bits ON and OFF. The thirteenth instruction, TM, is the most convenient for testing a single byte.

The following illustrates the use of AND's, OR's, and Exclusive OR's to manipulate bits:

1. *to turn selected bits OFF:* use an AND with a mask which has a corresponding 0 in the required bit positions, 1 elsewhere;
2. *to turn selected bits ON:* use an OR with a mask which has a corresponding 1 in the required bit positions, 0 elsewhere;
3. *to switch ON's to OFF's and OFF's to ON's:* use an Exclusive OR with a mask which has a corresponding 1 in the required bit positions, 0 elsewhere.

For the purpose of illustration, assume that B is a fullword, all zeros except for the last byte which has the form 0x10 10y1, where x and y may be either 0 or 1 (OFF or ON). Because bits are numbered beginning with 0, the x and y bits are, respectively, bits 25 and 30.

PROBLEM 1: Turn off bit 25 (if already OFF, leave it OFF). *Solution:* Let M be a fullword mask, all ones except at the end where it is 1011 1111; now use one of the AND instructions. For example, if both B and M are in core:

    NC   B,M

and the resulting B ends, as desired, in 0010 10y1.

PROBLEM 2: Turn on bit 30 (if already ON, leave it ON). *Solution:* Let M be a fullword mask, all zeros except at the end where it is 0000 0010; use one of the OR instructions. For example, if B and M are, respectively, in R8 and R12:

    OR   8,12

R8 now ends in 0x10 1010.

PROBLEM 3: Reverse the x and y bits, whatever they are. *Solution:* Assume B is in core:

    XI   B+3,X'42'

Note that X'42' is the same as B'01000010'. The bits opposite the ones in X'42' will cause reversals to occur.

PROBLEM 4: A fullword CODE in core has some of its bits defined as follows:

Wooden articles	bit 3 ON
Hardware	bit 9 ON
Notions	bit 28 ON

The code bits are placed as shown by question marks:

xxx? xxxx x?xx xxxx xxxx xxxx xxxx ?xxx

If the item is *either* wooden or a notion, the program is to branch to routine A. If the item is wooden *and* hardware, the program is to branch to routine B. Otherwise, the program goes to the next sequential instruction. The problem is to test bits 3, 9, and 28 and proceed on that basis. A possible flowchart (not the easiest way) is:

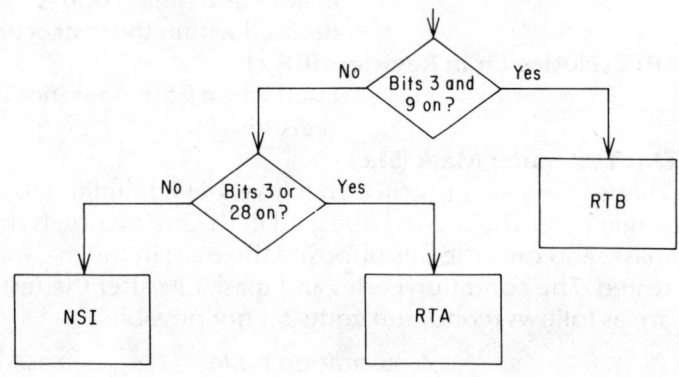

Possible masks, for testing, are:
Mask 1: 0001 0000 0000 0000 0000 0000 0000 1000 {Bits 3 or 28}
Mask 2: 1110 1111 1011 1111 {Bits 3 or 9}

For the decisions, the appropriate condition codes and mask bits are:

	condition code	mask bit
all zeros	0	8
not all zeros	1	4

For the possible program which follows, the areas of interest are:

TEST	DS	F
MASK1	DC	X'10000008'
MASK2	DC	X'EFBF'

The program steps, with explanations, are:

	MVC	TEST,CODE making a copy for the test
	OC	TEST(2),MASK2

The effect of ORing with MASK2 is to turn all the bits of the first two bytes ON except for bits 3 and 9. If these bits are already ON, then the first two bytes of TEST will be all ones. Unfortunately, zeros are needed. Then:

      XC   TEST(2),='FFFF'

switches all the bits in the first two bytes. Then:

      BC   8,RTB

takes care of the first decision. To continue:

	MVC	TEST,CODE making another copy
	NC	TEST,MASK1

The effect of ANDing with MASK1 is to turn all the bits OFF except bits 3 and 28. If *either* one is ON, then TEST will not be all zeros. Then:

	BC	4,RTA	if not all zeros, go to RTA

completes the program.

85. N: And (RX,c)

Used when the first operand is

Appendix for Instructions

86. NC: And in Core (SS1,c)
Used when both operands are areas in core.

87. NI: And Immediate (SI,c)
Used when the first operand is in core and the second is defined within the instruction.

88. NR: And in Registers (RR,c)
Used when both operands are registers.

89. O: Or (RX,c)
Used when the first operand is a register and the second an area in core.

90. OC: Or in Core (SS1,c)
Used when both operands are areas in core.

91. OI: Or Immediate (SI)
Used when the first operand is in core and the second is defined within the instruction.

92. OR: Or in Registers (RR,c)
Used when both operands are registers.

93. X: Exclusive Or (RX,c)
Used when the first operand is a register and the second is an area in core.

94: XC: Or in Core (SS1,c)
Used when both operands refer to areas in core; the instruction XC A,A always results in A equal to a string of binary zeros; this is useful for clearing a print area if the printer translates X'00' as a space.

95. XI: Exclusive Or Immediate (SI,c)
Used when the first operand is in core and the second is defined within the instruction.

96. XR: Exclusive Or in Registers (RR,c)
Used when both operands are registers.

97. TM: Test under Mask (SI,c)
This is a very easy instruction to use, but it is limited to a single byte. The second operand in the instruction is the mask, and only the bits opposite the ones in the mask are tested. The condition codes and mask bits after the testing are as follows (condition code 2 is not possible):

	condition code	mask bit
all zeros	0	8
mixed ones and zeros	1	4
all ones	3	1

The extended mnemonic instructions are even easier:
```
        BO      Branch if ones
        BM      Branch if mixed
        BZ      Branch if zeros
        BNO     Branch if not ones
```
Because the TM instruction is not destructive, no copy of the CODE (in Problem 4) need be made. The flowchart and program segment for this specific problem follow.

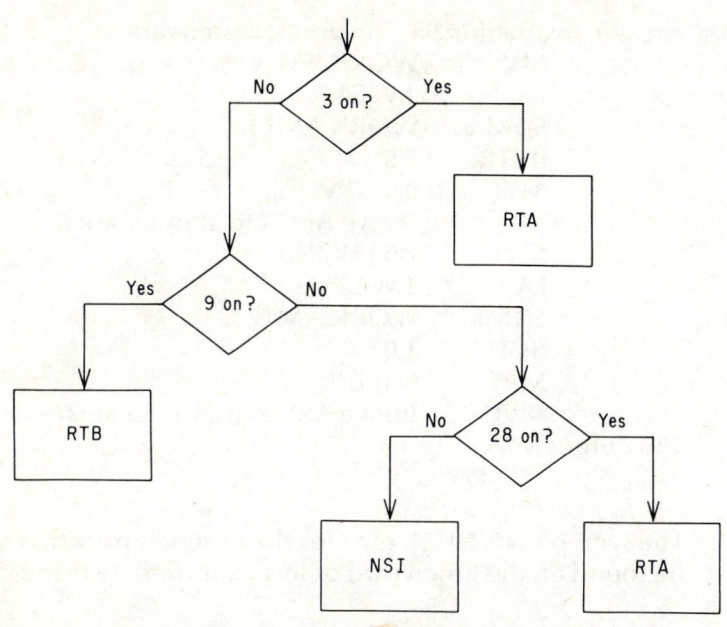

```
TM      CODE,B'00100000' or X'20'
BO      RTA
TM      CODE+1,B'01000000' or X'40'
BO      RTB
TM      CODE+3,B'00001000' or X'08'
BO      RTA
```

GROUP XIV. EDITING INSTRUCTIONS

98. ED: Edit (SS1,c)

Example: Given the numbers: 2,456.93 and -1.76, each expressed as a PL4:

```
AMT1 = 02 45 6ᴧ9 3C
AMT2 =       1ᴧ7 6D
```

Required: To express these numbers with asterisk fillers at the left.
Solution: Plan a pattern for the *longer* one:
```
02,456.93C
*dd,dd(.ddɸCR
```
Then the area designations are:
```
PAT     DC      XL13'5C20206B2020214B202040C3D9'
WORK    DS      XL13
```
The program steps are:
```
MVC     WORK,PAT
ED      WORK,AMT1
MVC     (to print area)
MVC     WORK,PAT
ED      WORK,AMT2
MVC     (to print area)
```
The results are:
```
*2,456.93
*****1.76 CR
```

99. EDMK: Edit and Mark (SS1,c)

Example 1 (Scientific): Use the same two numbers as in instruction 98.
Required: To print the numbers with blanks at the left and a minus sign, if necessary.
Solution: Plan a pattern for the *longer* one:
```
02,456.93C
ɸdd,dd(.dd
```
Then the area designations are:
```
PAT     DC      XL 10'40206B2020214B2020'
WORK    DS      XL10
```
The program steps are:
```
MVC     WORK,PAT
LA      1,WORK+7        placing the address
                        of the decimal point in R1 (required)
```

Appendix for Instructions

```
          EDMK    WORK,AMT1
          BNM     NM
          BCTR    1,0
          MVI     0(1),C'-'
    NM    MVC     (move AMT1 to another area)
          MVC     WORK,PAT
          LA      1,WORK+7
          EDMK    WORK,AMT2
          BNM     NM1
          BCTR    1,0
          MVI     0(1),C'-'
    NM1           (move AMT2 to another area)
```

The results are:
    2,456.93
    -1.76

Example 2 (Business): Use the same two numbers.
Required: To print a $ in front of each and CR if the amount is a credit (negative). The pattern and work areas are as in instruction 98. The program steps are:

```
    MVC     WORK,PAT
    LA      1,WORK+7
    EDMK    WORK,AMT1
    BCTR    1,0
    MVI     0(1),C'$'
    MVC     (move AMT1 to another area)
    MVC     WORK,PAT
    LA      1,WORK+7
    EDMK    WORK,AMT2
    BCTR    1,0
    MVI     0(1),C'$'
    MVC     (move AMT2 to another area)
```

The output is:
*$2,456.93
*****$1.76 CR

The symbols (40, 20, 21, etc.) for the different patterns can be found on the green card or in an appropriate manual.